ELECTIONS IN BRITAIN

R. L. LEONARD

Foreword by
David Butler

D. VAN NOSTRAND COMPANY LTD
LONDON
PRINCETON, NEW JERSEY TORONTO

For IRÈNE

D. VAN NOSTRAND COMPANY LTD.
Windsor House, 46 Victoria Street, London

D. VAN NOSTRAND COMPANY INC.
Princeton, New Jersey

VAN NOSTRAND REGIONAL OFFICES:
New York, Chicago, San Francisco

D. VAN NOSTRAND COMPANY (Canada) LTD.
Toronto

Published simultaneously in Canada by
D. VAN NOSTRAND COMPANY (Canada) LTD.

Library of Congress Catalog Card No. 67–27965

PRINTED IN GREAT BRITAIN BY
WESTERN PRINTING SERVICES LTD, BRISTOL

Contents

Foreword

THE IMPORTANCE OF ELECTIONS IS TAKEN FOR GRANTED BUT THE nature of elections is little understood. Nationwide voting every four or five years is an essential safeguard of democracy and liberty—that, at least, is an axiom of contemporary democratic faith. But there is remarkable ignorance on the vital questions: what do elections really accomplish? what factors decide elections? and even, how are elections conducted? Anyone who studies carefully the press reports on by-elections will be struck by the self-confident but quite unproven assertions about what matters in electioneering. Few reporters are bold enough to say that campaigning takes the form of a traditional and often empty ritual, which, like all rituals, has become surrounded by hallowed myths.

No one—not the politicians, nor the professional party workers, the pollsters or the psephologists—knows with any certainty what does decide elections. The experts are only really confident about some of the factors that have far less influence than is popularly supposed, or even no influence at all.

One of the reasons why I welcome Mr Leonard's lucid and reliable account of the electoral process in mid-twentieth century Britain is that, while it sets out so clearly what is beyond dispute, it does not pretend to answer the central questions to which there is, as yet, no definitive answer. Why do people stay loyal to their parties? why do they switch? what specific government or party policies or outside circumstances lead them to change or to change back their vote?

Politicians and journalists spend a great deal of effort planning or analyzing how votes may be influenced. The speculation on the subject is fascinating: sometimes it may hit on the truth but often it is far wide of the mark. Mr Leonard's book will help people to judge better than before between the rival theories that are propounded. It also has the down-to-earth virtue of providing the simplest and best account of the technicalities of electoral law and practise that I have encountered.

DAVID BUTLER

Nuffield College,
Oxford

Acknowledgments

The author wishes to thank the following authors and publishers for permission to reprint copyright material: Mr Alfred J. Junz and the Hansard Society for Table 3, which originally appeared in *The Student Guide to Parliament*; Mr Richard Rose and *The New Society* for Table 7; Mr D. E. Butler, Mr Anthony King, Mr Michael Steed and Macmillan & Co. Ltd for Tables 14, 15, 25 and 35, which are taken from *The British General Election of 1966*; Social Surveys (Gallup Poll) Ltd for Figure 8 and Table 19 and the information on which Tables 23 and 24 are based; Dr Mark Abrams and the *British Journal of Sociology* for Table 22, and the Liberal Party for the summary of election offences contained in Appendix 6.

He is greatly indebted to Mr Butler not only for contributing the foreword, but also for numerous helpful suggestions which have greatly improved the book in many particulars. Mr Anthony King also read the manuscript and contributed valuable advice. The responsibility for any errors remains that of the author alone.

The Glossary in Appendix 10 was compiled by Miss Norma Percy, formerly of Oberlin College and the London School of Economics.

1. Introduction

"THE DISADVANTAGE OF FREE ELECTIONS," MR MOLOTOV ONCE RE-marked to Ernest Bevin, "is that you can never be sure who is going to win them."

Perhaps, unconsciously, he had put his finger squarely on the feature which makes democratic systems of government so *interesting*. For it is the uncertainty which attends nearly every general election, at least in the United Kingdom, which adds spice to what might otherwise be regarded as a rather tiresome civic duty.

It is this, possibly, which explains a persistent paradox in British politics: that whereas only a tiny minority—probably less than 1 per cent—take an active part in politics between elections, well over three-quarters turn out to vote, without any compulsion, whenever a general election is held. Yet, the choice which is presented to the thirty million or so electors who record their votes at elections, is largely determined by the few thousands who take a continuing part in the activities of the political parties. It is they alone who participate in the selection of Parliamentary candidates and it is they who have a *direct* influence on the policies adopted by the political parties.

At most general elections about two million young men and women are entitled to vote for the first time. It was in the hope that it would be of assistance to some of them, and also to those older voters who are perhaps puzzled or uncertain about particular aspects of the electoral system, that before the 1964 general election the present author wrote a paperback entitled *Guide to the General Election*. It was intended to fill a gap which at that time seemed to exist for a book which explained the complexities of the electoral system in a simple manner and which also contained an account of how the political parties are organized, both locally and at national level, how their Parliamentary candidates are chosen and how the policies which they put before the electorate come to be adopted.

The reception which this book received was most encouraging, greatly exceeding the author's expectations, and a very considerable number of copies was sold. Shortly after the 1964 election the book went out of print and the author was urged to prepare a revised edition which would be equally relevant to future general elections. Moreover, it appeared that the book was being widely used as a textbook in universities on both sides of the Atlantic, as well as for civics courses in schools and adult educational colleges.

In the event, the revision has been more fundamental than at first appeared necessary—substantial alterations and additions have been made to nearly every chapter, and new chapters have been added on by-elections and local elections, on opinion polls and on the evolution of the system. The text has been brought completely up to date and several new appendices have been added. For the benefit of American and other non-British readers a glossary of terms which may be unfamiliar to them has been prepared. As the scope of the book has been changed and enlarged to such a considerable extent, it has been felt that a new title, more accurately reflecting its revised structure, is justified.

This book is addressed to voters who support all political parties and to those who remain uncommitted. The author is not lacking strong political opinions, but in this work he has attempted throughout to describe *how* the system works rather than explain *why* he approves or disapproves of its different features.

It should be emphasized that this work is an account of the British electoral system at the present time. It is not an historical work[1] or a general primer on the British constitution,[2] nor is it a work of comparative government.[3] Again for the benefit of non-British readers, however, it may be helpful to summarize in a few preliminary paragraphs the general characteristics of the British constitutional system in so far as it is relevant to elections.

1. The United Kingdom has a Parliamentary form of government. The Executive is not directly elected, but is formed from the membership of the Legislature. Ministers are members of the Legislature—the great majority, including those holding the leading offices, are members of the House of Commons. A minority are members of the House of Lords. This necessarily restricts the field

[1] See C. Seymour, *Electoral Reform in England and Wales* (New Haven, 1915); H. L. Morris, *Parliamentary Franchise Reform in England from 1885 to 1918* (New York, 1921); D. E. Butler, *The Electoral System in Britain since 1918* (Oxford University Press, 1963).

[2] See J. Harvey and L. Bather, *The British Constitution* (London, Macmillan, 1964).

[3] See *Parliaments and Electoral Systems* (London, Institute of Electoral Research, 1962); W. J. M. Mackenzie, *Free Elections* (London, Allen and Unwin, 1958) and Enid Lakeman and J. D. Lambert, *Voting in Democracies* (London, Faber, 1955).

of recruitment for ministers to a far greater extent than, for instance, in the United States of America.

2. It is, basically, a two-party system, though a third party, the Liberals, invariably polls a substantial vote and has a small representation in the House of Commons. An election campaign, therefore, like a debate in the House of Commons, is basically a confrontation between the Government and the Opposition. The party which wins a majority of the seats in the House of Commons forms a government and its leader becomes Prime Minister. Most elections produce a clear Parliamentary majority for one party or the other, though occasionally it is only a small one. Minority governments and coalitions are rare in peace time, and are unpopular with all parties.

3. The electoral system requires a single ballot and the candidate with the largest number of votes wins, even if he has polled only a minority of the total votes cast. This is sometimes known as the "first past the post" system. It is not a system of proportional representation, and it penalizes minority parties and inhibits their growth.

4. General elections in Britain are not held at fixed intervals, unlike in a majority of democratic countries. Though the maximum length of life of a single Parliament is five years, it may be dissolved at virtually any time at the wish of the Government. This gives the incumbent party a considerable advantage.

5. The United Kingdom has no written constitution; all laws, including electoral laws, may be changed by the passage of an Act of Parliament. It is technically easy, therefore, to change the electoral system at any time. In practice, only minor amendments are adopted with any frequency, and much of the present system is rooted in great antiquity.

2. When Elections are Held

APART FROM THE RESULT, THE PRINCIPAL UNCERTAINTY ABOUT A British general election is its timing. Unlike in the United States and the great majority of democratic states, outside the Commonwealth, there is no fixed date for British Parliamentary elections.

There is, however, a limit on the length of life of the House of Commons. In 1694 it was set at three years, which was increased to seven years in 1715. Under the Parliament Act of 1911 it was reduced to five years, which is the present limit. During both World Wars annual Prolongation of Parliament Acts were passed at the expiry of this limit to avoid the inconvenience of a war-time election, but though such a measure would theoretically be possible in peace-time it is inconceivable that it would be attempted.

No peace-time Parliament has in fact run its full five years, though that of 1959 came very close to it. Table 1 shows the length of each Parliament which has sat since 1918, the first to be elected under the 1911 Act.

Table 1

General Election	*Duration of Parliament*		*Original Government majority*
	Years	Days	
1918	3	265	263
1922	—	361	79
1923	—	266	None
1924	4	159	225
1929	2	105	None
1931	3	356	425
1935	9	200*	247
1945	4	189	186
1950	1	213	6
1951	3	183	16
1955	4	104	60
1959	4	342	100
1964	1	127	4
1966	?	?	97

*Duration extended by annual Acts of Parliament during 1939–45 war.

Except in the case of a minority government or one with a very small majority (as in 1950 and 1964) it will be seen that most

Parliaments have continued for a period of between three and four and a half years. Unless an election is precipitated by a Government defeat on a vote of confidence in the House of Commons (which has not occurred, otherwise than to a minority government, since 1886), it is in effect the Prime Minister who decides the date of a general election.

In theory the Sovereign may refuse the advice of the Prime Minister to dissolve Parliament. In practice she could not refuse any but the most frivolous request. Especially after a Parliament has passed its half-way mark, the Prime Minister may safely recommend a dissolution at any time.

The decision is his alone. In earlier times the agreement of the Cabinet was always sought, but in 1918 Lloyd George successfully set the precedent, which has never since been challenged, of not consulting his Cabinet on this decision. The Prime Minister may seek the advice of his senior colleagues, but is by no means bound by it. It is known that both in 1950 and in 1951, several senior Cabinet Ministers disagreed with Mr Attlee's decision to go to the country.

When there is a coalition government the Prime Minister has less freedom of choice in the matter, unless his own party actually possesses a majority in the House of Commons. Thus in 1945, the Labour and Liberal parties would have preferred an election to be deferred until October but the Prime Minister, Winston Churchill, insisted on a July election and his view prevailed.

Numerous factors influence prime ministers in their choice of general election dates. The economic situation, the state of the government's legislative programme in the House of Commons, the need for the country to be represented at important international negotiations by a government with a fresh mandate from the people or, if the government majority is precarious, as in the 1964 Parliament, the desire to increase its Parliamentary support. This list could be extended indefinitely, but there is little doubt that the principal factor was neatly summed up by Lord Poole, then joint chairman of the Conservative Party, in a speech at Newcastle in June 1963. "The Prime Minister is likely to have a general election," he said, "at the time when he thinks he is most likely to win it."

The Prime Minister's own prerogative of effectively choosing the date of general elections is a powerful weapon for the Government and a serious handicap to the Opposition. It has moreover assumed greater significance during the past decade when public opinion polls have provided a far more accurate and sensitive barometer to the relative standing of the political parties than existed in earlier periods. Traditionally, by-elections had been the main measure of political support, but the results of these can often be misleading. Thus in 1880, on the strength of two Conservative victories in by-elections at Liverpool and Southwark, Lord Beaconsfield went to the country, and saw his party go down to defeat.

Sir Anthony Eden (now Lord Avon) was, in 1955, the first Prime Minister to capitalize on the new precision with which public opinion polls enable a prime minister to choose a favourable moment for a dissolution, and subsequent prime ministers, notably Harold Macmillan and Harold Wilson, have followed in his footsteps. To have much hope of winning an election, under present conditions, it seems to be necessary for the Opposition party to lead the Government in popularity for three consecutive years, short of an error of judgment by the Prime Minister.

The advantage which "naming the day" gives to the Prime Minister has never been more apparent than during the 1964 to 1966 Parliament. Despite the Government's tiny majority, it remained clearly in command of the political situation, mainly because the opinion polls showed, almost continuously, that Labour was well ahead of the Conservatives in the country and could increase its Parliamentary majority almost at will. Partly because of his cautious nature, and partly because of non-electoral considerations, Harold Wilson waited until a highly encouraging by-election result[1] confirmed the opinion poll evidence—but there was then very little doubt that the ensuing general election would greatly augment his majority. The timing of general elections has become of crucial importance in British politics, as it is also in Australia, Canada and New Zealand where, too, the Government effectively chooses the date of general elections.

But though the Prime Minister's advantage appears immense, his area of choice is more limited than is immediately obvious. For, in practice, there are normally only a limited number of dates between which to choose.

The winter months are usually excluded from consideration for climatic reasons, April is reserved for Budget legislation, early May for local elections, Easter and Whitsun must be avoided and the period from mid-June to mid-September is the holiday season. This leaves early and late spring and early autumn as the only occasions normally seriously considered for electioneering. Apart from 1945, when the election was held on the earliest practicable date after the German surrender, 1950 and 1966 have been the only occasions

[1] See page 123, below.

since 1923 when the election has been other than in late May or October or early November. It may safely be assumed that the great majority of future general elections will take place in either May or October.

Table 2—Dates of General Elections

1924	Wednesday	29 October
1929	Thursday	30 May
1931	Tuesday	27 October
1935	Thursday	14 November
1945	Thursday	5 July
1950	Thursday	23 February
1951	Thursday	25 October
1955	Thursday	26 May
1959	Thursday	8 October
1964	Thursday	15 October
1966	Thursday	31 March

Over the last thirty years, general elections and the great majority of by-elections have been held on a Thursday, which is generally considered to be the least inconvenient day of the week for the purpose. There is no reason to believe that this practice will not continue. Before 1918, polling had been spread over a fortnight or more and results in the first constituencies to poll were already known when voters in other constituencies went to cast their votes. This was sometimes alleged to cause a "bandwagon" in favour of the party which made early gains. The only recent occasion when voting has been "staggered" was in 1945 when, because of local holiday arrangements, twenty-three seats in the north of England and Scotland polled one or two weeks later. But as none of the votes in this election were counted until three weeks after the original polling day, to allow for servicemen's votes to be sent from overseas, there was no risk of a "bandwagon" being created on that occasion.

Dissolution of Parliament is effected by Royal Proclamation, but it is customary for the Prime Minister personally to break the news with a statement giving notice of the dissolution.

In 1966, for example, the following statement was issued from 10 Downing Street on 28 February:

The Prime Minister has asked Her Majesty the Queen to proclaim the dissolution of Parliament. Her Majesty has been graciously pleased to signify that she will comply with this request. Dissolution will take place on Thursday, March 10. Polling will take place on Thursday, March 31.

The new Parliament will be summoned on Monday, April 18,

when the first business will be the election of the Speaker and the swearing in of Members. The new Parliament will be opened on Thursday, April 21.

Polling day is seventeen days (excluding Sundays and Bank holidays) after the date of dissolution, and by giving ten days' notice of dissolution, Mr Wilson's announcement came exactly one month before the election. This was ten days more than legally necessary, but it has become customary to give at least one month's notice of a general election.

In so far as the Government has the advantage of fore-knowledge in making its preparations, it may be presumed to gain by giving as short notice as possible. On the other hand, there is nowadays usually so much advanced Press speculation, that the Opposition is not likely to be caught napping.

As soon as Parliament is dissolved, the Lord Chancellor is ordered by Royal Proclamation to issue writs for the holding of fresh elections throughout the country. The writs are issued as soon as practicable following the Royal Proclamation and are sent to the Returning Officers in each Parliamentary constituency. The Returning Officer is the person appointed to organize the conduct of elections and in England he is normally the sheriff of the county, the mayor of the borough or the chairman of the urban district in which the constituency is situated. In Scotland he is the sheriff and in Northern Ireland the under sheriff. The Returning Officer appoints a Deputy Returning Officer, normally the Clerk of the Council, who in fact carries out most of the duties of the office.

Not later than four o'clock in the afternoon of the second day after the writ has been received the Returning Officer must publish, normally by means of posters outside public buildings and on commercial advertising sites, notices of election stating the place and times at which nomination papers must be delivered and the date of the poll. The election will only then be officially in train, though most people concerned in it will already have been extremely busy with their preparations for several weeks past.

3. The Voters

THE FRANCHISE IS ENJOYED BY ALL BRITISH SUBJECTS AND CITIZENS of the Republic of Ireland, with few exceptions, over the age of twenty-one. The only other qualification required is that of residence.

Thus, British Parliamentary elections are based on the principal of universal franchise. It was not always so, indeed it was only the abolition of plural voting (by university graduates and occupiers of business premises) by the Representation of the People Act of 1948, which finally established the principle of one man, one vote.

Like most developments in the British constitution, progress towards universal suffrage had been slow and gradual. Prior to 1832, voting was a privilege reserved for a mere 5 per cent of the population and it required five Acts of Parliament spread out over a period of one hundred and sixteen years for the transition from oligarchy to democracy to be effected.

The growth of the British electorate since 1832 is shown in Table 3 and Figure 1.

Apart from minors and aliens, the following categories of people are ineligible to vote:

Peers, or peeresses in their own right, who have not disclaimed their titles. Irish peers are entitled to vote, as are the wives of all peers.

Persons of unsound mind, who may, however, vote "during lucid intervals."

Felons. A person sentenced for treason or felony to a term of imprisonment exceeding twelve months is disqualified while serving his sentence.

Persons convicted of corrupt or illegal practices in connection with elections (see p. 92 below and Appendix 6) are ineligible to vote for five years from the date of conviction.

Although adults not in any of the above categories are qualified to vote they may not do so unless their names appear on the Register of Electors. This is prepared annually and the Registration Officer for each Parliamentary constituency is required by law to

Table 3—Growth of the Franchise

Representation of the People Acts	*Provisions relating to voters' qualifications*	*Total Electorate*	*Percentage of population over 20 years of age*
Prior to 1832	Counties—40s. freeholders. Boroughs—various and unequal franchises	509,000	5
1832	Counties—40s. freeholders, £10 copyholders, £10 leaseholders £50 tenants at will. Boroughs—£10 householders.	720,000	7
1867	Counties—40s. freeholders, £5 copyholders, £5 leaseholders, £12 tenants at will. Boroughs—All occupiers of rated dwelling houses, lodgers occupying £10 lodgings.	2,231,000	16
1884	Counties and Boroughs—A uniform franchise for householders and lodgers, giving a vote to every man over 21 who had a home.	4,965,000	28
1918	Men—Abolition of property qualification in counties. Qualification by either six months' residence or the occupation of a £10 business premises. Women—Enfranchised at the age of 30. Plural voting by university graduates and the holders of the business premises qualification restricted to two votes including the one for residence.	19,984,000	74
1928	Women enfranchised at 21. Male and female adult suffrage.	29,175,000	96·9
1948	University constituencies and all plural voting abolished. "One man—one vote."	34,915,000	96·7*

*The elimination of plural voting led to an apparent but not a real reduction in the percentage qualified to vote. This table is taken from *The Student Guide to Parliament* by Alfred J. Junz (London, Hansard Society, 1960).

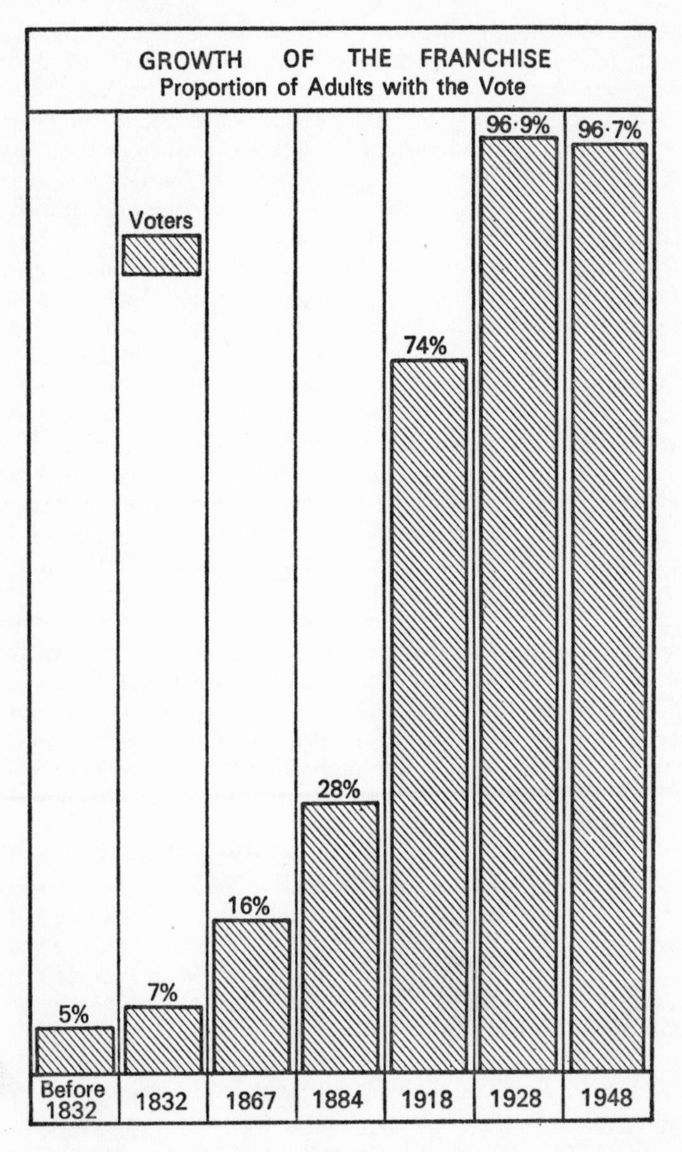
GROWTH OF THE FRANCHISE
Proportion of Adults with the Vote
Voters
5%
7%
16%
28%
74%
96·9%
96·7%
Before 1832
1832
1867
1884
1918
1928
1948

Figure 1

make "sufficient enquiry" to ensure that it is accurate. The Registration Officer is appointed by the Home Secretary and is normally the town clerk or the clerk to the council of the principal local government area (county or urban district) in which the constituency is situated. In Scotland the Registration Officer is the assessor of the county or large burgh of which the constituency forms part. The Registration Officer is the same person as the Deputy Returning Officer, who is responsible, in practice, for the organization of elections in the different constituencies.

To be included in the register one must be resident in a constituency on a qualifying date, 10 October, in England, Wales and Scotland. In Northern Ireland it is necessary to have been resident at the same address for three months before the qualifying date. This is to prevent residents of the Irish Republic crossing the border for a short period only and registering as voters. During weeks preceding the qualifying date the Registration Officer supplies forms, usually by means of a house-to-house canvass, to heads of households, requiring them to fill in details of all members of the household (including lodgers) who are eligible to vote.[1] Any person who refuses to comply or who gives false information is liable on summary conviction to a fine not exceeding £20.

In addition to eligible voters over the age of twenty-one on 10 October, persons whose twenty-first birthday occurs between then and the following 15 June should be included on the form. They will be registered as "Y" voters, but will be ineligible to vote at any election that takes place before the following 2 October. This means, in practice, that a high proportion of voters do not become eligible until nearer their twenty-second than their twenty-first birthdays.

A further special category are service voters. These are marked on the register with an initial "S" and, in addition to members of the armed forces, include persons employed in the service of the Crown outside the United Kingdom and the wives of service voters who are residing outside the United Kingdom to be with their husbands. Service voters are eligible to vote either by proxy or by post.

Non-resident occupiers or owners of business premises or land, whose rateable value is not less than £10 a year, are entitled to vote in local elections, providing they do not have a residential qualification in the same local government area. Since 1948, however, there have been no business voters in Parliamentary elections.

[1] Merchant seamen who think that they may have been left off a householder's form may obtain from a Merchant Marine Office a special form (*RPF 35*) on which they can apply directly for registration.

On 28 November each year a provisional register is published by the Registration Officer and is displayed in post offices, public libraries and other public offices until 16 December. The provisional register is in three parts. List A is the register already in force, compiled at the end of the preceding year. List B is the list of proposed additions to the register, consisting of newly qualified voters, those who have changed their addresses or those whose voting status has changed (*e.g.* by ceasing to be Y voters) from the previous year. List C is a list of proposed deletions from the register—consisting of those who have died or moved away or, again, those whose voting status has changed.

During the period that the provisional register is open to inspection claims and objections may be made to the Registration Officer, in respect of inaccurate entries or omissions. It is especially important that newly-qualified voters or those who have changed their address during the previous year should check that they are included in the provisional register; but there is no guarantee that voters who had been included in the previous years' register will be included in the next. If the head of the household has inadvertently failed to make an accurate return the voter might be included wrongly in the list of proposed deletions. There is also a possibility, on rare occasions, of a clerical error by the staff of the Registration Officer. The vast majority of voters who do not bother to check the provisional register each year nevertheless find, when they come to vote, that they have been properly registered. On the other hand, thousands of qualified voters at each general election find that they are not on the register and it is then too late to do anything about it.

Claims and objections may be made on or before 16 December (or 17th if the 16th is on a Sunday) on a form obtainable from the Registration Officer, who is entitled to make enquiries and to require proof of age or nationality from claimants.

The final register which consists of the former list A, with the entries from list B incorporated and those from list C removed, together with amendments arising from successful claims and objections, is printed shortly before 15 February, on which day it comes into force and remains valid until 14 February of the succeeding year. The Parliamentary register incorporates that used for local government elections, the franchise for which is, except for the difference explained on page 12, the same.[2] Copies of the register in each constituency are normally available for inspection in public libraries and certain other public offices, and free copies are provided for the agents of political parties and to Parliamentary

[2] Peers also are permitted to vote in local government elections.

candidates. Registers, or parts thereof, may also be purchased from the Registration Officer by members of the general public for 1s. plus one penny for every hundred, or part, names.

The register is divided into polling districts (each of which is distinguished on the register by an initial letter or letters). Polling districts are devised by the Registration Officer to give each voter the minimum distance practicable to travel to cast his vote. They vary in number between a mere handful of voters (sometimes less than a dozen) in remote hamlets to over 5,000 in densely populated areas in the centres of cities. The most usual number of electors in polling districts is, however, between 1,000 and 2,000. There are about 50,000 polling districts in the whole of the United Kingdom.

There are normally between one and a dozen polling districts in each Ward (the local government electoral area in towns), several of which normally comprise a borough constituency. In country areas each village would be a separate polling district and towns and larger villages would be subdivided. Within each polling district the electors are listed in street order, except in villages, where they are often listed alphabetically. Each entry consists of, reading from left to right, the voters' electoral number (counting from 1 in each polling district), his surname, first Christian name, the initials of any other Christian names and the number or name of the house. Within each household the names are given in alphabetical order, and there is no indication whether women are married or single.

Special categories of voters are indicated by letters printed in bold type immediately preceding the voter's surname, as follows:

Y—Young voters who may not vote in elections before 2 October.

S—Service voters.

L—not entitled to vote at Parliamentary elections.

C—not entitled to vote at county council elections.

R—not entitled to vote at rural district elections.

A bold J, printed, after the elector's name signifies that he is eligible for jury service.

A portion of the 1962 register for polling district N of the Millbank Ward of the Cities of London and Westminster constituency is reproduced in Figure 2.

Certain persons who would find it difficult or impossible to vote in person may claim the right to appoint a proxy or to vote by post. Full details of those who are eligible and of how to apply for postal and proxy votes are given in Appendix 3.

Applications for postal votes must be made, on the appropriate form, to the Returning Officer of the constituency at the latest by the twelfth day (excluding Sundays and public holidays) before the date of the poll. This is also the last day on which applications to cancel postal and proxy votes may be made. Applications by returning officers' staff and by constables may, however, be accepted by

	(Marsham Street, S.W.1)—*cont.*	
3974	Mallalieu, Betty M.	42
3975	Mallalieu, Edward L.	42
3976	Chapman, Edward J.—J	43
3977	Y—Chapman, Jacqueline M.	43
3978	Chapman, José E.	43
3979	Vickers, Joan H.	44
3980	Thornehill, Freda G.	45
3981	Ells, Dagnall G.	46
3982	Ells, Joan	46
3983	Morrissey, Kathleen	46
3984	Owen, Grace	47
3985	Owen, Humphrey F.—J	47
3986	Hamlyn, Ralph A.	48
3987	Hillingdon, (Lady) Sarah	49
3988	L—Hillingdon, (Lord)	49
3989	Channing, Lily M.	50
3990	Foster, Edwin T.—J	50
3991	Hubbert, David	51
3992	Hubbert, Eleanor	51
3993	Cunningham, (Sir) John	52
3994	Hannay, Dorothy M.	52
3995	Foord, Dorothy M.	55
3996	Foord, Edward J.—J	55
3997	Foord, Edward S.	55
3998	Owen, Violet	55
3999	Neilson, Ethel C.	56
4000	Neilson, George C.	56

Figure 2

the Returning Officer even after the twelfth day. It is highly advisable, however, for people eligible to vote by post to make arrangements well in advance. Delay can be experienced in obtaining the appropriate form and, where necessary, getting it signed by a doctor, and at every election many voters who would be eligible find that they have left it too late to apply. The importance of the postal vote, especially in closely contested constituencies, is touched on in Chapter 13, below.

In copies of the election register supplied to polling stations postal voters are marked in ink on the register with the letter "A" and voters with proxies are marked "B."

An absent voters list, including the addresses to which postal voting forms must be sent, is compiled by the Returning Officer and is available for inspection at his office. A copy of the list is supplied free of charge, on request, to each candidate or his election agent.

Although considerable efforts are made by Registration Officers to ensure the accuracy of the election register, it is an imperfect instrument. It is already four months old when published and sixteen months old at the end of its life. Thus at all times large numbers of dead people are on the register while people who have moved are not registered in respect of their current address (probably only a minority of these apply for a postal vote or travel back to their previous neighbourhoods to register their votes on polling day).

Some years ago the Government Social Survey made a study of the accuracy of the election register. They found that when compiled it was 96 per cent accurate (*i.e.* 96 per cent of electors were registered in respect of the address in which they were actually living on the qualifying date). By the time the register was published it was only 94 per cent accurate. There was thereafter a cumulative loss of $\frac{1}{2}$ per cent per month, due to removals, until at the last month that the register was in force its degree of accuracy was only 87 per cent.[3]

The 1948 Representation of the People Act provided for two registers to be compiled each year, but in 1949 as an economy measure the number was reduced to one. The apparent effect of this has been to disfranchise anything up to an additional 3 to 4 per cent of the population at any one time.

A proposal to produce a constantly up-to-date register, with the aid of computer techniques, was considered by the Speaker's Conference on Electoral Law in 1965–66 (see page 159 below). The conference recommended that a study of its feasibility should be made. If this proves fruitful it should for the first time be possible to register virtually 100 per cent of the eligible voters.

Citizens of Commonwealth countries resident in the United Kingdom are regarded as British subjects and are entitled to vote, as are Irish citizens. Relatively few Commonwealth immigrants have, in the past, availed themselves of this opportunity.

There are a number of reasons for this. Many of the immigrants, particularly those from Asian countries, speak little or no English and may be ignorant of their rights. Some of them come from coun-

[3] See P. G. Gray, T. Corlett and Pamela Frankland, *The register of electors as a sampling frame* (London, Central Office of Information, 1950). A more recent survey showed similar results. See P. G. Gray and Francis A. Gee, *Electoral Registration for Parliamentary Elections* (London, Government Social Survey, 1967).

tries with authoritarian forms of government, and are strangers to the phenomenon of voting. Others regard their stay in Britain as a purely temporary affair and take no interest in British politics.

Moreover, many Commonwealth immigrants live in crowded and sub-standard housing, and their landlords may be reluctant to advertise the extent of the overcrowding by listing tenants in the election register. All in all, it seems probable that in the recent past fewer than half of the Commonwealth immigrants have been registered, and that, of those registered, only a minority have recorded their votes.[4]

The total number of registered voters is now over 36 million, including nearly 300,000 Y voters and about 300,000 service voters. Over 31 million are in England and Wales, 3½ million are in Scotland and 900,000 in Northern Ireland.

Over 27 million, or 75·8 per cent, actually voted in the 1966 election. The largest turn-out ever was in 1950, when 28¾ million, 84 per cent of the registered voters, went to the polls. The turn-out in 1966 was the lowest since 1945.

[4] See Nicholas Deakin (ed.), *Colour and the British Electorate 1964* (London, Pall Mall Press, 1965), for a detailed account of the participation of Commonwealth immigrants in British electoral politics. In 1966 there was a considerable increase in the proportion of immigrants on the register.

4. Constituencies

THE HOUSE OF COMMONS HAS AT PRESENT 630 MEMBERS, EACH OF whom is the representative of a single-member constituency. The origin of the different constituencies is diverse. Some constituency names, particularly those comprising medium-sized provincial towns, go back several hundred years, though the precise boundaries of the constituencies are unlikely not to have been altered at some time. The large majority of constituencies have in fact been delineated within the last twenty years.

The basis of representation in the House of Commons was, with few exceptions, two members for each county and two for each borough from 1264 to 1832. No attempt, however, was made to ensure that members represented equal numbers of voters and enormous discrepancies in the size of constituencies had developed long before the 1832 Reform Act. Medieval boroughs which had declined almost to nothing retained their right to elect two members, while large cities such as Manchester, Leeds, Sheffield and Birmingham, which had grown up during the seventeenth and eighteenth centuries, had no separate representation. It has been estimated that by 1832 the largest Parliamentary constituency had more than one hundred times as many electors as the smallest. In 1832 and again in 1867 the worst anomalies were removed, but no systematic attempt was made to redraw the electoral map on the basis of approximately equal constituencies.

In 1885 a much more thorough redistribution was undertaken and the ratio between the largest and smallest constituency was reduced to 8 : 1. The Representation of the People Act of 1918 went one stage further and reduced the disparity to a maximum of 5 : 1. The 1885 Act also replaced the great majority of two-member constituencies with single-member seats, though the last of the two-member constituencies did not disappear until 1950.

Although the principle of approximately equal constituencies had been accepted in 1918, no provision was made to correct anomalies caused by future movements of population. Thus, by 1939, the rapid growth of suburban fringes to London and other major cities had produced a large number of constituencies with an excessive number of electors, while depopulation of city centres and of remote rural areas had left many other constituencies with tiny electorates.

The Speaker's Conference on Electoral Reform in 1944 recommended the establishment of permanent machinery for the redistribution of seats, so that major anomalies should not again arise. An Act of the same year established four Boundary Commissions, one each for England, Wales, Scotland and Northern Ireland which should make a general review of constituency boundaries at intervals of not less than three nor more than seven years. Each commission consists of three members and each is chaired by the Speaker of the House of Commons, though his role is largely nominal.

The first reports of the commissions were, with one major amendment (mentioned below), approved by the House of Commons in 1948 and came into effect at the 1950 general election. They provided the first systematic delineation of constituencies which had ever been attempted, and of the 625 seats which made up the 1950 Parliament only eighty had retained their boundaries untouched.

In November 1954 the Commissions produced their second reports which came into force in time for the 1955 general election. The recommendations which they made were much less far-reaching than in 1948. Altogether, major alterations were suggested to 172 constituencies and minor alterations to forty-three, and the creation of five additional seats was recommended.

The proposals of the commissions, and particularly those of the English Commissions, were greeted with a storm of protest. There was general agreement, with which the commissions themselves concurred, that if redistribution had previously been too infrequent it now erred very much on the other side.

Two groups of people were particularly incensed by the effects of this second redistribution within barely five years—Members of Parliament and active party workers in the constituencies. MPs of all parties were agreed that the normal hazards of political life were severe enough, without adding the further hurdle of a fresh bout of redistribution every five years or so. For a stiff hurdle it proved in a number of cases: safe seats were to become marginal or even hopeless, and marginal seats might become safe for the other side.

In 1950, of the seventy members who lost their seats at least half could blame redistribution, partly or wholly for their defeat. In 1955 at least eleven members were in the same position. Sir Frank Soskice (Labour) and Sir Ralph Assheton (Conservative) were double casualties, losing their seats through redistribution on both occasions.

The inconvenience which redistribution brings to members of local political organizations was well described by Sir Kenneth Thompson, then Conservative MP for Liverpool, Walton, in a speech in the House of Commons on 15 December 1954. He said:

We in the House are compelled to face the facts of political life. Political party organization consists of the little constituency club, a polling district committee, a ward organization, a constituency organization all pyramiding up from the modest humble, unobtrusive men and women who... do the slogging day-to-day work of a political party.... Every time a unit is taken from the electorate of a constituency, every time a boundary line is altered by however much or however little, some Mrs Jones is chivvied out of this organization and hived off to what is to her a foreign land, where there are a lot of people who do not speak her language. At the whim—if that is not an offensive word—of the Boundary Commission, she is expected to accept this as her lot and destiny and the pattern of her future political activity.[1]

The strong reaction to the 1955 redistribution led to amending legislation being passed by the House of Commons in 1958 which extended the period between general reviews of constituencies to a minimum of ten and a maximum of fifteen years. This meant that the next general review had to take place no earlier than the end of 1964 and no later than the end of 1969. Early in 1965 the Boundary Commissioners announced that they were commencing a general review, and their final reports should be ready well within the time laid down. The power to make recommendations at any time has been maintained.

The statutory rules under which the commissions operate are few and simple. The total electorate is divided by the number of constituencies to secure an electoral quota, and the number of electors in each constituency should "be as near to the quota as is practicable." Boundaries of local government areas should be respected but may be crossed if necessary to avoid "excessive disparities" from the quota. However, the commissions might depart from the rules "if special geographical conditions, including in particular the size, shape and accessibility of a constituency, appear to them to render a departure desirable." The number of constituencies in Scotland and Wales must not be less than seventy-one and thirty-

[1] Quoted by D. E. Butler in an article "The Redistribution of Seats," *Public Administration*, Summer 1955, which is much the fullest account of the procedure and effects of redistribution yet to appear. See also *The Electoral System in Britain since 1918, op. cit.*, by the same author.

five respectively and in Great Britain not substantially greater or less than 613, while Northern Ireland is to have twelve seats.

This allocation gives more than their proportionate share of seats to Scotland and Wales, presumably as a sop to their national susceptibilities; conversely Northern Ireland has less than its proportionate share, because its domestic affairs are dealt with by the Northern Ireland Parliament at Stormont.

Of the 630 seats in the present Parliament 511 are in England, thirty-six in Wales, seventy-one in Scotland and twelve in Northern Ireland. At the 1966 general election the largest constituency Antrim South (in Northern Ireland) had an electorate of 113,645—five times as large as the smallest, the Western Isles (in Scotland) with an electorate of 22,823. In England the largest constituency, Billericay, with 102,198 electors, was over four times more populous than the smallest—Birmingham, Ladywood—with 25,294.

The rapid growth of new towns and housing estates in recent years has led to a considerable expansion of the electorates of certain constituencies and it is surprising that the English Boundary Commission has not made interim recommendations to create a handful of extra seats before the next general review of constituencies. In 1955, for instance, no constituency outside Northern Ireland had more than 80,000 voters—by 1959 there were two and by 1966 no fewer than nineteen, with several pushing the 100,000 mark. At the same time the smallest seats were getting smaller, and a number of constituencies in decaying city centres had begun to challenge the traditionally sparsely populated Scottish Highland seats for the dubious honour of having the smallest electorate.

The political impartiality of the Boundary Commissions is unquestioned, but their work certainly has a considerable effect on the

Table 4—Changes in the electorate in certain large and small constituencies

	1955	1959	1966
Billericay	58,872	78,328	102,198
Epping	68,184	83,647	97,645
Portsmouth, Langstone	68,299	79,885	96,166
Cheadle	61,626	71,205	91,893
Hornchurch	77,041	87,544	90,969
Hitchin	62,258	75,493	90,840
Manchester, Exchange	52,376	47,067	26,400
Merioneth	27,472	26,435	25,395
Birmingham, Ladywood	46,904	39,131	25,294
Orkney and Zetland	27,868	26,435	24,927
Ross and Cromarty	25,750	25,350	24,530
Glasgow, Kelvingrove	39,672	34,319	24,299
Western Isles	24,856	25,178	22,823

fortunes of the political parties and some of their decisions, and particularly those of the English Commission, have been the cause of fierce controversy.

Until 1948 there was an accidental pro-Labour bias in the electoral system. The effect of this was that the Labour Party needed to poll fewer votes than the Conservatives to secure any given number of seats in the House of Commons. Thus in the 1929 general election Labour polled 266,981 fewer votes than the Conservatives, but secured twenty-eight more seats. As a result of the 1948 redistribution the pro-Labour bias disappeared and a similar bias in favour of the Conservatives was introduced into the system. Accordingly, in the 1951 general election the Labour Party obtained over 200,000 more votes than the Conservatives, but had twenty-six fewer seats in the House, and the Conservatives were able to form the government. This bias continued to manifest itself in the 1955 and 1959 general elections, when it was estimated that Labour needed to gain 1·4 per cent more of the total vote in order to gain an equal number of seats to the Conservatives. But in the 1964 and 1966 elections the bias disappeared, perhaps because of movements of population in the years since 1959.[2]

To some extent the anti-Labour bias is fortuitous, due to the heavy concentration of Labour voters in mining and other predominantly industrial areas, while the Conservative vote is more evenly spread out.[3] This disadvantage was, however, compounded by the action of the English Boundary Commission, which decided in 1948, without any statutory authority, to give preferential treatment to rural voters in comparison with urban on the grounds of the "advantages of accessibility and convenience" enjoyed by the latter. This led them to recommend county constituencies with an average electorate of only 55,360 voters, while their recommended borough constituencies had an average electorate of 61,442.

When these recommendations were debated by the House of Commons Mr Attlee's government proposed the creation of seventeen extra borough seats, which lowered the average borough electorate to 57,833—though this meant that borough constituencies

[2] In his appendix to *The British General Election of 1964*, by D. E. Butler and Anthony King (London, Macmillan, 1965), pp. 357–58, however, Michael Steed argues that the bias against Labour may still exist, and that its apparent disappearance in 1964 and 1966 was due to the lower turn-out in those elections. See also *The British General Election of 1966*, by Butler and King (London, Macmillan, 1966), pp. 319–21.

[3] See Andrew Hacker, "Some votes are more equal than others," *New Society*, 13 February, 1964.

still had over 2,000 more voters on average than county seats. In 1954–55 the English Commission's report, approved *in toto* by the House of Commons, further widened this differential to nearly 4,000. As the Conservatives are stronger in rural areas and Labour in the towns this action of the English Boundary Commission, however well-intentioned, had unfortunate political effects. While there is a good case for a small number of thinly populated counties in North Wales and the north of Scotland to receive special treatment in order that the physical size of constituencies should not become so enormous as to make the task of representing them almost impossible, there is surely no justification for a general discrimination against the urban voter.

In fairness to the commissions it must be said that the political effects of their recommendations cannot always be accurately predicted. In 1948 it was widely anticipated that the Conservatives would gain considerably from the proposed changes and this did indeed prove to be the case. In 1954–55 it was again anticipated that the Conservatives would benefit (and the late Aneurin Bevan accused them of gerrymandering; an accusation which Sir Winston Churchill had made against Labour, with even less justification, in 1948), but when the results of the 1955 general election were analyzed it was apparent that the political effect of redistribution had been so negligible that it was impossible to determine which party had benefited.[4]

While detailed criticism can be made of the recommendations and procedures of the Boundary Commissions,[5] in general the difficult problem of delineating constituencies appears to have been solved more satisfactorily in Britain than in many other countries and accusations of gerrymandering are rare.

All Parliamentary constituencies are now territorial ones, though from 1603 to 1950 representatives of the universities (elected by post by graduates) sat in the House of Commons. University representation was abolished, in accordance with the principle of "One man, one vote," by the Labour Government of 1945–51. This step was opposed by the Conservative Party at the time and a pledge to restore the university seats was given by Sir Winston Churchill. When a Conservative government was elected, in 1951, however, no attempt was made to redeem that pledge, and two

[4] See D. E. Butler, *The British General Election of 1955* (London, Macmillan, 1955), p. 157.

[5] See in particular J. F. S. Ross, *Elections and Electors* (London, Eyre and Spottiswoode, 1955); and D. E. Butler, *The Electoral System in Britain since 1918, op. cit.*

years later Sir Winston announced that the question was to be dropped.

The method of election within each constituency is the simplest yet devised. Each voter has one vote which he records by marking an X against the candidate of his choice on the ballot paper. The candidate who polls the largest number of votes in the constituency is elected, even if he is supported by only a minority of the voters. Where three or more candidates are in the field this is of course quite a common occurrence, and in the 1966 general election 181 out of 630 Members were elected with a minority vote.

Where support for three candidates is very evenly balanced it is possible for a member to be elected with not much more than one-third of the votes, as happened in the Caithness and Sutherland constituency in 1945, when the result was as follows:

E. L. Gander Dower (Con.)	5,564	(33·47%)
R. McInnes (Lab.)	5,558	(33·43%)
Sir A. Sinclair (Lib.)	5,503	(33·10%)
Cons. majority	6	

A more recent example was the South Dorset by-election in November 1962. Here the result was:

Guy Barnett (Lab.)	13,783	(33·5%)
Angus Maude (Con.)	13,079	(31·8%)
L. Norbury-Williams (Lib.)	8,910	(21·7%)
Sir Piers Debenham (Ind.)	5,057	(12·3%)
Paul Burn (Ex-serviceman)	181	(0·7%)
Michael Fudge (Ex-serviceman)	82	
J. C. O'Connor (Ex-serviceman)	45	
Lab. majority	704	

It is of course theoretically possible in multi-sided contests for a candidate to be elected with considerably less than one-third of the votes. This has, however, never happened, at least in modern times, though in a by-election for the former Combined English Universities constituency in 1947, contested by five candidates, the winning Conservative polled just over 30 per cent of the votes.

The combination of single-member constituencies and a "first past the post" method of voting leads to considerable discrepancies between the proportion of votes polled by parties and the number of seats which their candidates obtain in the House of Commons. Between the two larger parties this normally has the effect of exaggerating the majority obtained by the more successful and thus ensuring a larger majority for the government in the House of

Commons than could mathematically be justified. The only recent occasions when this has not occurred were in 1950 and 1951 when, in closely contested elections, the bias against the Labour Party, described above on p. 22, offset the tendency of the system to favour the larger party. Had the Labour lead in votes been a little larger on these two occasions Labour would undoubtedly have benefited from this tendency. The proportions of votes and of seats won by the three main parties since 1945 are shown in Table 5.

Table 5—Percentage of seats and votes won by the parties

	1945		*1950*		*1951*		*1955*		*1959*		*1964*		*1966*	
	votes	*seats*	*votes*	*seats*	*votes*	*seats*	*votes*	*seats*	*votes*	*seats*	*votes*	*seats*	*votes*	*seats*
Labour	48·1	62·2	46·1	50·4	48·8	47·2	46·4	44·0	43·8	40·9	44·1	50·3	47·9	57·6
Conservative	40·2	33·2	43·5	47·7	48·0	51·3	49·7	54·5	49·4	57·9	43·4	48·1	41·9	40·2
Liberal	9·0	1·9	9·1	1·4	2·5	1·0	2·7	1·0	5·9	1·0	11·2	1·4	8·5	1·9

It is clear from a glance at the Liberal performance that third parties are very much under-represented under present conditions. They are likely to remain so unless they poll at least 30 per cent of the total vote or their support is concentrated in regions or individual constituencies, instead of being fairly evenly distributed throughout the country as has been the case with the Liberals.

The apparent injustice of the system led to demands in the period before the First World War for the introduction of a system of proportional representation (or PR), as practised in a number of other countries. The only system which ever enjoyed much support among British opinion is that of the single transferable vote in multi-member constituencies (returning, say, three to seven members). Under this system, if in a six-member constituency the Conservative candidates polled half the votes, the Labour candidates a third and the Liberals a sixth the Conservatives would get three seats, Labour two and the Liberals one. Over the country as a whole this system would still tend to benefit large parties and penalize small ones, but to a lesser extent than does the present system.

Proportional representation was almost adopted in 1918, but support for it thereafter rapidly declined except, understandably, in the Liberal Party. Since the Second World War, however, the Liberals have tacitly conceded that they are unlikely to rally popular support for this measure and it is no longer a major item in their programme. Although various systems of PR work perfectly effectively in a number of countries (Ireland, West Germany, Sweden, etc.), it is extremely unlikely that it will ever be adopted in Britain where coalition government, which seems to be the inevitable concomitant of PR, is heartily disliked in peace time. The truth is that only small parties, which are heavily penalized under the present system, are likely to favour PR. If one of them became a large party, with the prospect of power, it would clearly be doing so well under the present system that it would be likely to lose its enthusiasm for change. This is, in effect, what actually happened in the case of the Labour Party which fifty years ago tended to support PR.

A less drastic reform of the voting system, the alternative vote, was actually approved by the House of Commons both in 1918 and 1931. This provided for single-member constituencies, but if the leading candidate polled only a minority of the votes the lowest candidate would drop out and his second preference votes would be transferred until the winner emerged with more than 50 per cent of the votes. But defeat of the measure in the Lords in 1931, followed by a change of government prevented it coming into force.

Both PR and the alternative vote were considered anew in 1965–67 by the Speaker's Conference on Electoral Law (see Chapter 20, below), which decided, however, by a margin of nineteen votes to one, to recommend no change in the present system.[6]

Although in recent general elections every one of the 630 constituencies has been contested the real battle is invariably confined to a much smaller number of seats. More than half the seats are so securely held by one or the other party that their loss is almost inconceivable. The number of constituencies which actually change hands at each general election is usually quite small. In 1966, fifty-four seats changed hands, in 1964, seventy and in 1959, only thirty-five. Even in 1945, a "landslide" year, only 227 seats changed hands out of 640, little more than a third.

This figure must represent virtually the maximum number of seats at all likely to change hands at any one general election. Far more frequently it is to be expected that less than one hundred seats would change hands, but at most elections one hundred gains for the opposition party would be more than enough to ensure victory. (Up to 1945, it was usual for a larger number of seats to change

[6] Cmnd. 3202, February 1967. For a more detailed account of PR and other systems of voting see articles by the present author in the *Guardian*, 19 July, 1965 and the *Statist*, 15 October, 1965. See also Lakeman and Lambert, *Voting in Democracies*, *op. cit.*

hands at general elections, but there are few signs of a return to such conditions.)

In practice, constituencies are regarded as falling into three categories: safe, hopeless and marginal. A safe seat held by one party is of course a hopeless seat for the other. Of the 630 seats in the present House of Commons about 400 may reasonably be regarded as safe for one side or the other. It is impossible to give the exact definition of a safe seat, but a reasonable working assumption is that any constituency with a majority of 6,000 or more (or about 14 per cent of the votes cast) is unlikely to change hands at a general election.[7] In the average size constituency the loss of such a majority would mean that more than seven voters out of every hundred had changed their minds in the same direction. Such a heavy turnover of votes is unusual in British conditions.

There are, however, well over 200 seats where the majority is below 6,000. These are the marginal seats which are won or lost at general elections, and as the general trend in all constituencies is normally in the same direction it is singularly unlikely that more than half of these would in fact change hands at any particular general election. Given the small movement of opinion at recent general elections it is in fact only those with a majority of less than 3,000–4,000 (about 10 per cent of the votes cast) which have appeared to be seriously marginal at any one election.

In recent years it has become common practice to convert the voting figures in constituency contests into percentages. This enables the "swing" to be calculated. The term "swing" was first applied to elections by David Butler. It is defined as the average of one party's gain and another's loss. Thus, if at one election the Conservatives poll 50 per cent of the votes and Labour 45 per cent and at the next election the figures are reversed, there has been a swing to Labour of 5 per cent. (If both parties lose to a third it is calculated by taking half the difference between the two parties' losses, *e.g.* if at one election the Conservatives poll 60 per cent and Labour 40 per cent and at the next the Conservatives poll 50 per cent, Labour 38 per cent and the Liberals 12 per cent, the net swing from Conservative to Labour is 4 per cent.)

The utility of the swing concept is that it enables the overall

[7] The only ones to have done so since 1945 are Darlington, in 1951, Glasgow, Pollock, in 1964 and Cheadle, in 1966. In by-elections more dramatic changes are liable to occur. In 1962 three constituencies with majorities larger than this changed hands—Orpington, Middlesbrough West and South Dorset—as did Leyton in 1965 and Walthamstow West and Hamilton in 1967.

change in a constituency between two elections to be expressed in a single figure, and thus allows easy comparison between the results in different constituencies. Table 6 shows an example from the 1966 general election.

Table 6—Voting figures in Gravesend, 1964 and 1966

	1966		*1964*	
Labour	30,276	(49·8)	26,074	(45·4)
Conservative	25,484	(41·9)	25,326	(44·1)
Liberal	5,092	(8·4)	6,015	(10·5)
Lab. maj.	4,792	(7·9)	748	(1·3)
Swing to Lab.		3·3		

The Labour percentage vote in Gravesend rose by 4·4 per cent, and the Conservative percentage fell by 2·2 per cent, making a swing to Labour of 3·3 per cent. With this figure one can tell at a glance that Labour did better in Gravesend than in the country at large, where the average swing to Labour was 2·7 per cent. Making further comparisons, one discovers that in two of the neighbouring constituencies to Gravesend—Gillingham and Sevenoaks—there was an identical swing to Labour, 3·3 per cent, but that in a third neighbour, Rochester and Chatham, the swing to Labour was only 1·1 per cent.

While the important contest in the great majority of constituencies has for the past forty years been between the Labour and Conservative candidates there are a few constituencies where this has not been the case. There have in recent general elections been about twenty constituencies in which Liberal Members have been elected or in which Liberal candidates have represented a strong challenge to the sitting member. There are also three constituencies in Northern Ireland which have been represented in recent Parliaments by Irish Nationalist Members of one type or another. The other nine Northern Ireland constituencies are safe Conservative seats, but in several of these, too, the main opposition is provided not by the Labour Party but by the Nationalists.[8]

Nothing is static in British politics and over the years safe seats have become marginal and marginal ones safe. This is due partly to the movement of population, partly to the effect of redistribution and partly to changes in political opinion. Each new Parliament elected alters the status of different constituencies. In the 1966

[8] Nationalist candidates in Wales and Scotland also have run strongly in recent by-elections, capturing seats at Carmarthen in July 1966 and Hamilton in November 1967.

general election the Labour Party made a net gain of forty-eight seats. But the effect on the electoral map was far greater than this. The great majority of safe Labour seats became yet safer, some Labour marginals moved into the safe category, some Conservative marginals became Labour marginals, hitherto safe Conservative seats became marginal and safe Tory seats had reduced majorities. If the Conservatives were to win the next general election this whole pattern would be reversed.

5. Political Parties—National

ALTHOUGH THEIR EXISTENCE IS IGNORED IN VIRTUALLY ALL THE LAWS and regulations governing the conduct of elections, it is the political parties which give them shape and purpose. The overwhelming majority of Parliamentary candidates are party adherents, and it is an exceptionally rare event for an independent candidate to secure election.

In this chapter and the next the organization of each of the three major parties, together with that of minor parties who have put up candidates in recent general elections, is examined in some detail. Before discussing the individual parties it should be noted that there is a common pattern in the organization of all three parties.

Each party is made up of three elements—the Parliamentary Party, comprising the MPs and peers who belong to the party concerned, the party bureaucracy and the mass membership throughout the country. The third element is discussed in Chapter 6, the first two are dealt with here.

Of these three elements it is the Parliamentary Party which is dominant in each party. This is explicitly recognized in the Conservative Party and also, though to a lesser degree, in the Liberal Party. In both these parties strong Parliamentary groups existed long before either a bureaucracy or a mass membership organization was formed. The latter were set up, in the mid nineteenth century specifically to provide support for the Parliamentary party and to ensure the continued election of MPs representing the party concerned. In the Labour Party the mass organization was set up first. In the early days of this century when there were only a few Labour MPs they were clearly subordinate to the extra-Parliamentary organization of the party. But, at least from 1924 onwards, when the first minority Labour government was formed, the Parliamentary Labour Party has secured for itself in practice, though not formally, a dominance comparable to that of the Parliamentary Conservative Party and superior to that of the Parliamentary Liberal Party.

In all three parties then, it is the leader of the party in the House of Commons who is recognized as the leader of the whole party, even though the other elements in the party have had no direct part in the election of the leader. The members of the Parliamentary Party—full-time professional politicians in daily contact with each other for eight months of the year—have little difficulty in monopolizing the most important party decisions.

In the past this was less true of the Labour Party, particularly when it was in opposition, but even here it is fair to say that it was only when there was crucial division within the Parliamentary Party that the views of non-Members of Parliament, as expressed through the party conference, began to count and occasionally to prevail. Since 1960–61, however, when Hugh Gaitskell successfully challenged and later reversed the Labour Party conference decision on defence policy, the pre-eminence of the Parliamentary Labour Party, in policy matters, has become very apparent. When a party forms the government, of course, much of the authority of the Parliamentary Party is assumed by the Cabinet, whose influence far outweighs that of any organ of the party.

The party bureaucracy in the Conservative Party is under the direct control of the leader. In the Labour and Liberal parties it is responsible to the elected representatives of the mass membership. Because many of these elected representatives are also Members of Parliament the Parliamentary Party exercises a considerable indirect influence over the bureaucracy, and clashes of interest are rare. It is undoubtedly true that responsibility for the party machine is much more widely diffused in the Labour and Liberal parties, in practice as well as in theory, than in the Conservative Party.

The party bureaucracy consists of a headquarters in London and a series of regional offices throughout the country. The Conservative and Labour headquarters face each other from different sides of Smith Square in Westminster—the Conservative headquarters is called the Central Office, the Labour one Transport House. This is actually the headquarters of the Transport and General Workers' Union, the Labour Party being tenants of part of the building. The Liberal Party headquarters has, since 1965, also been situated in Smith Square. The nearness of all three headquarters to the House of Commons emphasizes their close relationship to their respective Parliamentary parties.

The functions of the party bureaucracy are manifold. They are responsible for publishing a constant stream of pamphlets and leaflets for distribution through the constituency and local branches of the party. These range from the crudest propaganda handouts to sophisticated discussion pamphlets on policy, intended for the use of study groups within the party. Posters and other propaganda material are also produced in great quantities, and a steady supply of advice and information is supplied to constituency party secretaries who seldom experience a week without receiving at least one communication from head office.

Each party maintains a research department, one of the important functions of which, especially when the party is in opposition, is to brief its spokesmen in the House of Commons on the wide range of subjects on which they are called upon to speak. This department is also responsible for much of the material contained in the party publications, though it is the publicity department which actually prepares them.

The publicity departments of the Conservative and Labour parties, as well as looking after party publications and Press enquiries, are responsible for the expensive advertising campaigns which are now an important feature of the "run-up" period to a general election.

An increasingly important function in recent years has been the supervision of the party television and radio broadcasts and both the Labour and Conservative parties maintain a mock television studio in which their MPs and prospective candidates can be put through their paces. The bureaucracy is also responsible for organizing speaking tours by prominent MPs and supplying speakers on demand for a very large number of speaking engagements throughout the country, both at election time and between elections.

The organization department, which is responsible for maintaining an efficient vote-winning machine throughout the country, is the least glamorous but perhaps the most essential section of the party headquarters. The organizing staff, through its regional offices, keeps a fairly tight rein on the full-time constituency agents, although most of these are actually employed by the constituency parties. Not only is the organization department concerned that the constituency and local parties should be in a constant state of readiness to fight elections, it is also responsible for ensuring that the selection of Parliamentary candidates proceeds according to the party rules. If there is any irregularity it is their function to bring the constituency party into line.

Other head office departments deal with such matters as local government, international and Commonwealth affairs (including relations with like-minded political parties in other countries), and the raising of funds.

Although each party headquarters undertakes the same tasks, the efficiency with which they are performed varies considerably. The Conservative Party not only has a much larger staff, but because it pays considerably higher salaries is able to attract better qualified people to its employ and enjoys a far lower turnover of employees than the Labour Party. The Liberal Party's staff is substantially smaller than that of the Labour Party, but its salary scales are rather higher, though less than those of the Conservatives.

Table 7 shows how the size of the staff of the three parties varies and is a rough guide to the thoroughness with which they are able to perform their tasks. It was published originally in *The New Society*, 8 August 1963, and although the actual figures are no longer correct the general picture which it conveys is still valid.

Table 7—The Staffs of the Parties

	Conservatives Eng. and Wales		*Labour Britain*		*Liberals Eng. and Wales*	
	A	C	A	C	A	C
General HQ Staff	39	86	12	45	5	22
Agents						
National office	9	12	7	9	3	3
Regional offices	60	60	38	24	10	10
Constituencies	520	?	208*†	?	64*†	?
Research	25‡	17	12	6	4	3
Publicity	24†	28	9*†	5	3	2

*Plus part-time volunteers.
†Plus paid part-time staff.
‡Independent of general headquarters.

A=administrative

The maintenance of the party bureaucracy is an expensive business and the difference in the size of the staffs of the three parties is undoubtedly a direct reflection of their financial resources.

The most recently published balance sheet of the Labour Party shows the annual income for 1965–66 as £379,000. In the same year the Liberal Party income was some £66,000 and its expenditure, £92,000.[1] The Conservative Party resolutely refused to publish its accounts, but its income clearly cannot be less than double that of the Labour Party and probably is several times larger.[2] The Companies Act, 1967, clause 18 of which obliges companies to reveal political and charitable gifts of more than £50, will go a long way

[1] In addition, the Scottish Liberal Party had an income and expenditure in 1965–66 of some £8,500.

[2] The annual income of the Conservative Central Office during the period 1960–64 has been estimated at about £2,250,000, of which £800,000 "was almost certainly raised from large business firms." See Richard Rose, *Influencing Voters* (London, Faber, 1967), p. 263. These figures, like the published ones for the Labour and Liberal parties, refer only to the income of the national party organization. The finances of local parties are discussed on pp. 60–61, below.

to remove the secrecy which hitherto has shrouded Tory finances.[8]

The party bureaucracy is entrusted with the task of organizing the annual party conference which provides the sole opportunity for the members of the mass organization to give collective expression of their views. The three conferences are held in rapid succession, first Liberal, then Labour, then Conservative, in September and October each year at one of the small number of seaside resorts which have the facilities to house such a gathering. The most popular are Blackpool, Scarborough, Brighton and Llandudno. Each conference receives a report on the work of the party bureaucracy during the year and a Parliamentary report, and then proceeds to debate a large number of policy resolutions which have been sent in by constituency parties or, at the Labour conference, by trade unions.

The Conservative conference is a cumbrous affair with some 4,500 delegates and acts as little more than a party rally. It has no formal power to do more than proffer "advice" to the leader, and the number of occasions when it has had any apparent influence on party policy is extremely small. But there are signs that things are changing, particularly since the election of Edward Heath as leader of the Conservative Party. Mr. Heath, unlike all his predecessors, attends throughout the conference and appears to take its deliberations seriously.

The Labour Party conference has about 1,200 delegates of whom about half come from constituency parties, and the remainder mostly from trade unions. As the constituency delegates represent less than one million members while the trade unionists represent over five million, the latter have a predominating influence on the voting, though spokesmen from the constituency parties enjoy the lion's share of the speech making. It is the Labour Party conference which decides the policy of the party and especially the election programme on which it is to fight. Theoretically, therefore, its influence is immense. In practice, however, the Parliamentary leadership consistently enjoys the support of several of the larger trade unions and this normally guarantees it a majority at the conference. It is only when one or more of the normally "loyalist" trade unions disagrees with the Parliamentary leadership, as happened on the issue of defence policy in 1960, that the leadership runs a serious risk of defeat.

The majority of delegates to a Labour Party conference undoubtedly sincerely believe that they are there to frame the policy

[8] In the autumn of 1967 the Conservatives announced that in future they would publish their annual accounts.

of the party and the debates are vigorous and lively. And the great amount of time and trouble which both the Parliamentary leadership and many busy trade union leaders devote to the conference is strong evidence that its influence, though less than decisive, is far from negligible.

The Liberal Assembly has in theory considerably less power than the Labour Party conference. However, the absence of a trade union block vote and the small number of Liberal MPs means that the Parliamentary leadership of the Liberal Party is in a far weaker position in relation to its party conference, and this undoubtedly increases the influence of the conference. Although on paper the Liberal Assembly has little more power than the Conservative conference, in practice its influence on its Parliamentary leadership is at least as strong as that of the Labour Party conference. When a party is in Government the power and prestige of Ministers inevitably detracts from the influence of the party conference; this is true of all parties.

Since the early 1960's the party conferences have received extensive coverage on television, and this has to a great extent modified their function. They are now regarded as excellent "shop windows" for the parties' leadership and policies; in 1966, for instance, it was widely noticed that the opinion poll rating of each of the three parties improved sharply in the period immediately after its conference.[4] Conversely, of course, if a party conference were to be fractious or quarrelsome, as was often the case with the Labour Party during the 1950's, it might well result in a sharp fall in the party's popularity.

The Conservative and Unionist Party is the oldest and most resilient of British parties. Its origins go back at least 300 years to Stuart times and the earlier name, Tory Party (still widely used by friends and foes alike), dates from 1679. "Tory" was an Irish word meaning brigand, and it was applied to the King's supporters, who were supposedly willing to use Irish troops against Englishmen to enforce the succession of James II. Tories were supporters of the Crown and drew their support principally from the squirearchy and the clergy.

The name Conservative was adopted following the Reform Act of 1832. Some thirty years later, finding themselves in a permanent minority in the then politically dominant urban middle class, the party, under the inspiration of Benjamin Disraeli (later Lord Beaconsfield) set out to form the basis of a mass party. Local Conservative associations were formed in many constituencies to secure

[4] See, in particular, *Daily Telegraph*, 20 October, 1966.

the election of Conservative MPs. The 1867 Reform Act, which gave the vote to most of the urban working class, gave added impetus to this development and in the following three years the party took on substantially its present shape.

The Liberal Unionists, who broke away from the Liberal Party in 1886 because of their opposition to Irish Home Rule, finally amalgamated with the Conservative Party in 1912, hence its present unwieldy name.

Conservatives in Scotland and in Northern Ireland normally call themselves Unionists and Ulster Unionists respectively, but the term is infrequently used in England and Wales.

Three distinct elements make up the modern Conservative Party. The Parliamentary Party, the National Union and the Central Office. They are linked at the apex by the leader, who enjoys very considerable formal power, much more than his Labour or Liberal counterparts. The most influential of the three elements is undoubtedly the Parliamentary Party, which is composed of all Members of Parliament who take the Conservative Whip. The management of the Parliamentary Party is the responsibility of the Chief Whip, who is appointed by the leader of the party.

From the Parliamentary Party and the Conservative peers, the leader chooses his Cabinet when a Conservative government is in power; when in opposition he appoints a "shadow cabinet" and a deputy leader.

The Parliamentary Party has a number of specialist committees on defence, foreign affairs, trade and industry, agriculture, etc. When the party is in opposition the committees are attended by both front and back bench Members, when in government they are comprised entirely of back bench Members.

An unofficial body which wields considerable power is the "1922 Committee" (known as such because it was originally formed on the initiative of the back bench Members elected to the Parliament of 1922). This committee, known formally as the Conservative Members' Committee, meets every week while Parliament is sitting and consists, when a Conservative government is in power, of all the Conservative back bench Members. Its chairman, who is elected by the committee, is a prominent back bencher and his is a most influential voice in Party affairs. When Conservatives are in opposition the 1922 Committee comprises the entire Parliamentary Party, and the back bench influence is diluted by the presence of the leading front bench Members.

The National Union of Conservative and Unionist Associations, which dates from 1867, is the body representing the mass following

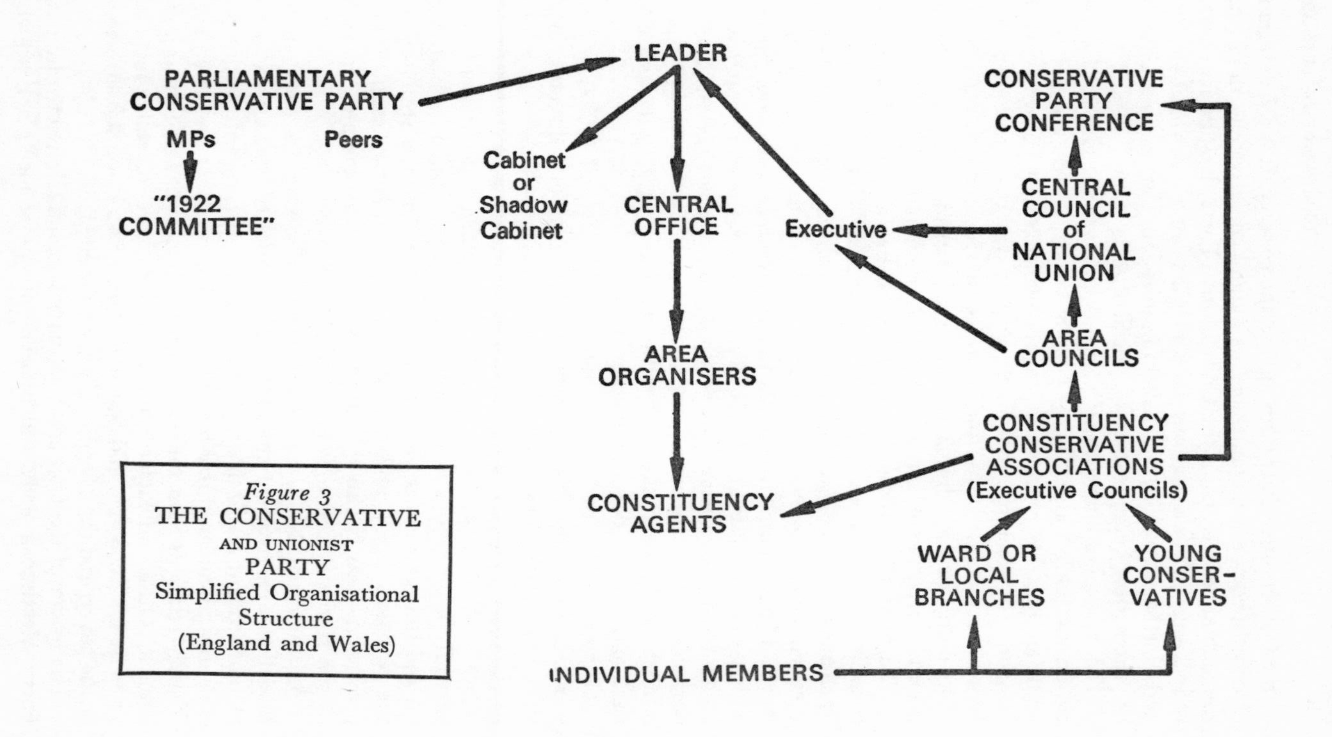

Figure 3
THE CONSERVATIVE AND UNIONIST PARTY
Simplified Organisational Structure
(England and Wales)

of the Conservative Party throughout the country. It is a federation of constituency associations, and its annual conference is, in effect, the annual conference of the Conservative Party. Despite its name, it includes only associations in constituencies in England, Wales and Northern Ireland; a parallel organization, the Scottish Unionist Association, being responsible for Scotland.

The governing body of the National Union is the Central Council, an unwieldy body of some 3,000 members, on which every constituency has five representatives and which meets once a year in London. Its executive committee, with about 150 members meets about every two months, and is an important political body. Most of its more routine administrative work is normally delegated to its general purposes sub-committee, which meets monthly.

The executive of the National Union has a series of advisory committees on various aspects of organization—local government, Parliamentary candidates, Young Conservatives, women, etc.—and these committees are normally reproduced at area and constituency levels. The National Union has twelve provincial area councils on which the constituency associations are directly represented and which meet once a year. The National Union is not responsible for organization—its function is to act as a two-way channel of communication between the leader, the Parliamentary Party and the rank and file members in the constituencies.

Organization is the responsibility of the Central Office, which was established by Disraeli personally in 1870. Its direction has since remained firmly under the control of the leader who appoints its chairman (normally a Cabinet Minister or leading Parliamentary figure) and other officers. The general director of the Conservative Central Office, who is responsible to the chairman and is, in effect, his full-time deputy, is also traditionally the honorary secretary of the National Union and the Central Office agent in each of the provincial areas is also the honorary secretary of the area council of the National Union.

An unofficial body, the Bow Group (founded in 1957), and modelled, to a great extent, on the Fabian Society, does a great deal of independent research on policy matters. Although its members, who are all under thirty-five, are all Conservatives and it enjoys friendly relations with the party organization, it has no formal link with it. Other unofficial groups, formed more recently, include Pressure for Economic and Social Toryism (PEST), on the left wing of the party, and the Monday Club, on the right.

The leader of the Conservative Party is nominally elected by the Party Meeting, a body which never otherwise meets and which consists of all the Conservative Members of the House of Commons and of the House of Lords, all prospective Parliamentary candidates and the executive committee of the National Union. In fact, until 1965, there had never been a contested election, the leadership being decided by a process of informal consultation between the leading party figures in both Houses of Parliament and only one name was put before the meeting for formal endorsement.

When a Conservative Government was in power the Sovereign was normally advised to send for whoever was designated, even before the meeting to elect the new leader had been convened. On the resignation of Sir Anthony Eden in January 1957, the Queen was advised by Sir Winston Churchill and Lord Salisbury to send for Harold Macmillan, in preference to R. A. Butler, as the new Conservative Prime Minister. This process of involving the Sovereign in the selection of a political leader was widely criticized at the time, and some Conservatives felt that on future occasions their leader should be chosen by vote. But no change was effected and when, in October 1963, Harold Macmillan announced his forthcoming resignation in the midst of the Conservative conference, ten days of the most intensive canvassing and speculation ever known in British politics ensued before the Queen, on the advice of the retiring Prime Minister, sent for the Earl of Home; the most fancied candidate, R. A. Butler, having again been passed over.

Although Lord Home was quickly accepted by the majority of the party the degree of dissatisfaction at the manner of his selection was far greater than ever before. Following the Conservative defeat in the 1966 general election, Sir Alec Douglas-Home (as Lord Home was then known) instituted a one-man enquiry—carried out by the then party chairman, Lord Blakenham—into alternative methods of selecting the leader of the party. Upon receiving Blakenham's report, Sir Alec announced, on his own authority, that in future the leader would be chosen by a ballot of Conservative MPs.

The system he laid down had no exact parallel, and it was clearly devised to assist the evolution of a compromise choice should there be a sharp division between two controversial and mutually incompatible candidates. Under the new system a candidate needs to secure on the first ballot not only an absolute majority, but a lead of 15 per cent over his nearest rival. If the first ballot fails to produce a winner, a second ballot is held for which new nominations may be made. To be successful on the second ballot, a candidate needs only an absolute majority. If the second ballot is inconclusive a third and final ballot is held. The names on the ballot paper would be those of the three leading candidates in the second ballot.

Voters are required to indicate their second as well as their first preference. The candidate with the smallest number of first preferences is eliminated and his second preferences are distributed between the other two. The winner of this ballot is then presented formally to the Party Meeting for election as party leader.[5]

When Sir Alec resigned, in July 1965, the new system was put into effect. Three candidates were nominated, and on the first ballot Edward Heath received 150 votes, Reginald Maudling 133 and Enoch Powell fifteen. Heath had received an absolute majority, but his lead over Maudling was less than 15 per cent and a second ballot was therefore necessary. However, both Maudling and Powell declined re-nomination, and Edward Heath was elected unopposed. Once elected, the leader has, in theory, an enviable security of tenure. He is not required to submit himself for periodic re-election and remains in office until his death or resignation.[6]

The Conservative Party has always been one of the two principal parties of the State. In the period from 1832 to 1916 Conservative and Liberal governments alternated in power, though the Liberals had the lion's share of office. Since then the Conservatives became used to being the normal "government party" and held power either separately or in coalition for all but nine of the forty-eight years between 1916 and 1964. Their defeats in the general elections of 1964 and 1966 confronted them with the prospect of a long period in opposition, a role in which they are patently unhappy.

The Conservative Party has not published membership figures for some years, but it is believed to have between two and three million members. It is organized in each of the 630 constituencies and in both the 1966 and 1964 general elections it nominated 629 candidates, contesting every seat except that represented by the Speaker of the House of Commons.

The *Labour Party* differs from all others in possessing a large affiliated membership (mostly trade unionists) in addition to its individual members. In fact for the first eighteen years of its existence it was impossible to become an individual member of the Labour Party.

The party was formed, under the title of the Labour Representa-

[5] For the full text of the new procedure see Anthony King (ed.), *British Politics: People, Parties and Parliament* (Boston, D. C. Heath and Hammond, 1966), pp. 169–70.

[6] R. T. McKenzie, however, argues that, in practice, Conservative leaders have enjoyed less security than their Labour counterparts who have had to offer themselves for annual re-election. See *British Political Parties*, second edition (London, Heinemann, 1963).

tion Committee, at a conference in London on 27 February 1900. The conference was convened by the Trades Union Congress, following a resolution passed at the TUC conference the previous year. It was attended by representatives of sixty-seven trade unions and three small socialist organizations (the Independent Labour Party, the Social Democratic Federation and the Fabian Society). The purpose of the organization established at this meeting was to secure the representation of "working-class opinion" in the House of Commons "by men sympathetic with the aims and demands of the Labour movement." In the early years the Labour Representation Committee (which became the Labour Party in 1906) did no more than co-ordinate the political activities of its affiliated organizations and all Labour candidates at that time were financially sponsored by one or other of these affiliates.

Success at first came slowly to the new party. Only two Labour MPs were elected in the 1900 election (one being J. Keir Hardie who had been the driving force behind the creation of the party). But in the period from 1906 to 1923 the Labour Party progressively replaced the Liberals as one of the two principal parties, becoming the official Opposition in 1922 and forming its first (minority) government in 1924.

In 1918 the party adopted a new constitution which, with a number of subsequent amendments, is still in force today. This at last made provision for individual membership of the party and the creation of constituency Labour parties throughout the country followed immediately after. The 1918 constitution also specifically committed the party for the first time to Socialist objectives.

The Parliamentary Labour Party is made up of Labour MPs and Peers, though the latter are relatively few in number and wield little influence. Each year when Labour is in opposition it elects, by ballot, a leader, deputy leader, Chief Whip, and a Parliamentary committee (or Shadow Cabinet) of twelve members in the Commons and three in the Lords. Unlike in the Conservative Party, whenever a vacancy occurred for the leadership it has invariably been contested. On the last occasion, in February 1963, Harold Wilson obtained 115 votes, George Brown eighty-eight and James Callaghan forty-one, on the first ballot. As no candidate had obtained a clear majority, a second ballot was held between the two leading candidates, and Harold Wilson emerged as the leader by 144 votes to 103. Once a leader has been elected he may find, as did Clement Attlee (leader from 1935 to 1955), that he is never challenged for re-election. On the other hand, Hugh Gaitskell (leader from 1955 to 1963), was challenged both in 1960 and 1961. It is

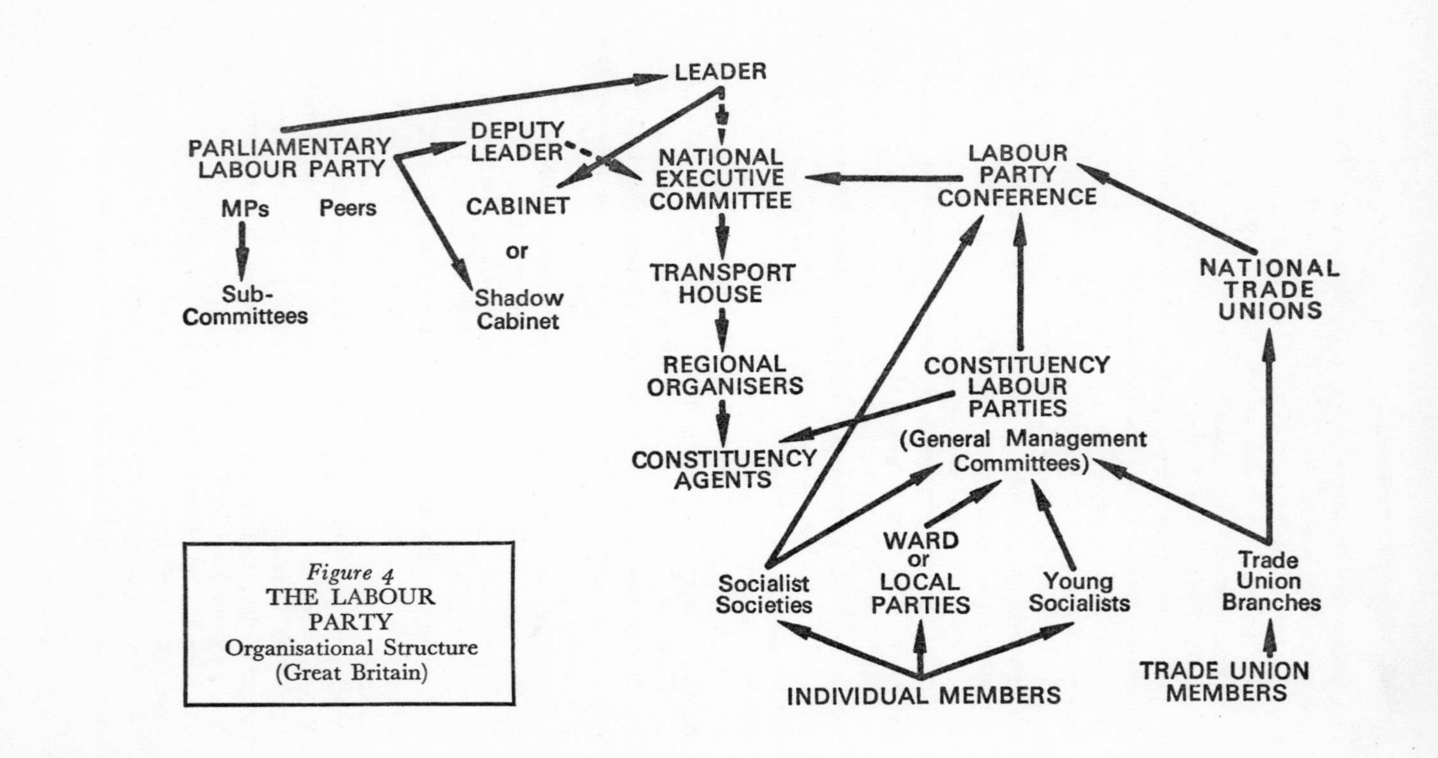

Figure 4
THE LABOUR PARTY
Organisational Structure
(Great Britain)

clear, therefore, that the leader of the Labour Party enjoys less security of tenure, at least in theory, than his Conservative counterpart and his powers are certainly less. When in government, however, Labour does not require its leader or other officers to offer themselves for annual re-election and the leader, as Prime Minister, appoints his own Cabinet. In government, therefore, a Labour leader is no less clearly in command than his Conservative counterpart.

The leader of the party is also, when in opposition, chairman of the Parliamentary Party and presides at its weekly meetings. Policy and Parliamentary tactics are discussed at these meetings and are frequently put to the vote, which is binding on the leader and the Parliamentary committee. When Labour is in government the Parliamentary Labour Party elects a back bench Member as chairman and it comes to resemble more closely the Conservative 1922 Committee, though Ministers are entitled to attend and to vote, and frequently do so. A regular interchange of views between a Labour Government and its back bench supporters takes place through the "Liaison Committee." This consists of the chairman of the Parliamentary Labour Party, two elected vice-chairmen—also back benchers—and an elected representative of the Labour peers, with the Chief Whip and the Leader of the House of Commons representing the Government.

The party bureaucracy is not controlled, as in the case of the Conservative Party, by the leader, but by a National Executive Committee elected by the Labour Party conference.

This committee, normally known as the NEC, consists of twenty-eight members of whom twenty-six are elected by the conference. The other two are the leader and deputy leader of the Parliamentary Labour Party, and their *ex-officio* membership of the NEC is the only direct link which the Parliamentary Party has with the party organization as a whole. Of the twenty-six elected members of the NEC, twelve are elected by the trade union delegates to the conference, seven by the constituency party delegates and one by the delegates of socialist and co-operative organizations. Five women members and the treasurer are elected by the whole conference, but as the trade unionists' votes predominate, the constituency party delegates have little influence on the election of these six members. In practice, a majority both of the seven constituency party representatives and the five women members have invariably been Members of Parliament.

The NEC, which normally meets monthly, appoints the general secretary who is the chief official of the party and who is responsible to them for the running of Transport House and of the party machine in the country. The NEC and its various sub-committees are also responsible for making appointments to other senior posts in the party bureaucracy.

In 1965 the Labour Party had 817,000 individual members and 5,602,000 affiliated members. The latter belonged to seventy-nine trade unions which had affiliated nationally to the party, one Co-operative Society (the Royal Arsenal) and five small socialist organizations (the Fabian Society, the Jewish Socialist Labour Party (Poale Zion), the Socialist Educational Association, the Socialist Medical Association and the Society of Labour Lawyers).

Among the affiliated trade unions are the traditional "big six"—the Transport and General Workers' Union, the Amalgamated Engineering Union, the National Union of General and Municipal Workers, the National Union of Mineworkers, the Union of Shop, Distributive and Allied Workers and the National Union of Railwaymen, and most of the other larger unions representing manual workers. The most important unions not affiliated to the Labour Party all represent white collar or professional workers, *e.g.* the Civil Service unions, the National Union of Teachers and the National and Local Government Officers (NALGO). Some white collar unions, such as the Clerical and Administrative Workers' Union are, however, affiliated to the party.

The unions pay an affiliation fee of 1s. per member per year, the same sum as is paid to the national party by constituency Labour parties. As the affiliated membership is so much larger, however, the unions contribute by far the larger part of the party's funds at national level. The affiliation fees are not paid from the general funds of the union but, by law, must come out of a special political fund from which members may contract out if they do not wish to support the Labour Party financially. The political levy, as it is called, usually amounts to about fourpence a month and it is paid by just over four-fifths of the members of the affiliated trade unions.

The Fabian Society, which has been affiliated to the party from the beginning, is an independent socialist research organization, whose principal function is the publication of books and pamphlets studying current political, economic, and social problems from a democratic socialist viewpoint. Although it is an affiliated body it expresses no collective viewpoint within the party and in practice its relationship to it is very similar to that of the Bow Group to the Conservative Party. The Fabian Society, founded in 1884, restricts its membership to those "eligible for membership of the Labour Party." This means, in effect, that non-members of the Labour

Party may join, provided they are not members of other political parties.

Dissatisfaction had been expressed within the Labour Party for many years that the efficiency of the party machine was in many respects inferior to that of the Conservatives and that no comprehensive review of the party constitution had taken place since 1918. In 1965 a rank-and-file campaign, entitled Plan for an Efficient Party, began to organize support for reform. As a result of this pressure the NEC agreed at the 1966 party conference to set up a commission of enquiry, from among its own members, to review the organization and constitution.[7] It is therefore possible that extensive changes may result within a few years.

Although it has been one of the two major parties since 1922, the Labour Party has until recently been markedly less successful than the Conservatives in securing office. In 1945 Labour was returned with a large majority in the House of Commons and formed a government which continued in office, introducing major legislative changes in a great many fields until the general election of October 1951. For thirteen years after 1951 Labour was in opposition, but in 1964 it snatched a narrow victory over the Conservatives which was consolidated in the 1966 general election.

Minority Labour governments were in power in 1924 and in 1929–31, dependent on Liberal support in the House of Commons. Labour Ministers also took part in the wartime coalition governments of 1916–18 and 1940–45. For all the rest of its life the Labour Party has been in opposition, and this factor is undoubtedly reflected in its constitution which, unlike that of the Conservatives, is more fitted to a party in opposition than in government.

The Labour Party normally contests every seat at general elections, except for a few county constituencies in Northern Ireland.

The *Co-operative Party*, founded in 1917, has been formally allied to the Labour Party since 1926. It has agreed not to put up candidates in opposition to Labour candidates and the only Co-operative nominees who are put forward are those selected by constituency Labour parties as Labour candidates. They are normally designated as Co-operative and Labour candidates, but otherwise are indistinguishable from other Labour candidates. The Co-operative Party has branches in more than half the Parliamentary constituencies. Co-operative Societies with eleven million members are affiliated to the party, but it is doubtful whether it has more than 5,000 individual members. It sponsors its candidates financially in

[7] See *Interim Report of the Committee of Enquiry into Party Organisation* (London, the Labour Party, 1967).

the same way as the trade unions (see Chapter 7). Its local branches are affiliated to constituency Labour parties, and it is financed more by contributions from the political funds of Co-operative Societies than by the subscriptions of its members.

In 1959 the Co-operative Party agreed with the Labour Party to limit the number of its sponsored candidates to a maximum of thirty. The table below shows the number who have been nominated at recent general elections.

Table 8—Co-operative Party candidates

Year	*Candidates*	*Elected*
1945	33	23
1950	33	18
1951	37	16
1955	38	18
1959	30	16
1964	27	19
1966	24	18

The *Liberal Party* has roots which go back as far as those of the Conservatives. It grew out of the old Whig Party, which dated from the debates in 1679 over the attempted exclusion of the Duke of York, later James II, from the succession. The Whigs probably derived their name, which was at first meant contemptuously, from the Whiggamores, a body of Scottish Presbyterian insurgents who had marched on Edinburgh in 1648. The Whigs became identified as the party of those wishing to assert the authority of Parliament over that of the Sovereign and, later, as the advocates of Parliamentary reform through extension of the franchise. In the years following the Reform Act of 1832 the new name of Liberal Party gradually replaced the old. Unlike "Tory," the term "Whig" passed completely out of common usage by the end of the century.

Under the leadership, successively of Palmerston and Gladstone, the Liberal Party dominated the Parliamentary scene during the greater part of the Victorian era. In 1886, however, it suffered a major setback through the defection of the Liberal Unionists over the issue of Irish Home Rule. In 1906 a Liberal government was elected with an immense majority, but during the next fifteen years the Liberals were replaced by the Labour Party as one of the two main parties, a process which was aided by a bitter division between the supporters of the last two Liberal Prime Ministers, Asquith and Lloyd George. The decline of the Liberal Party continued unabated until the early 1950s when it was reduced to a mere six seats in the House of Commons. Since then it has periodically shown signs of

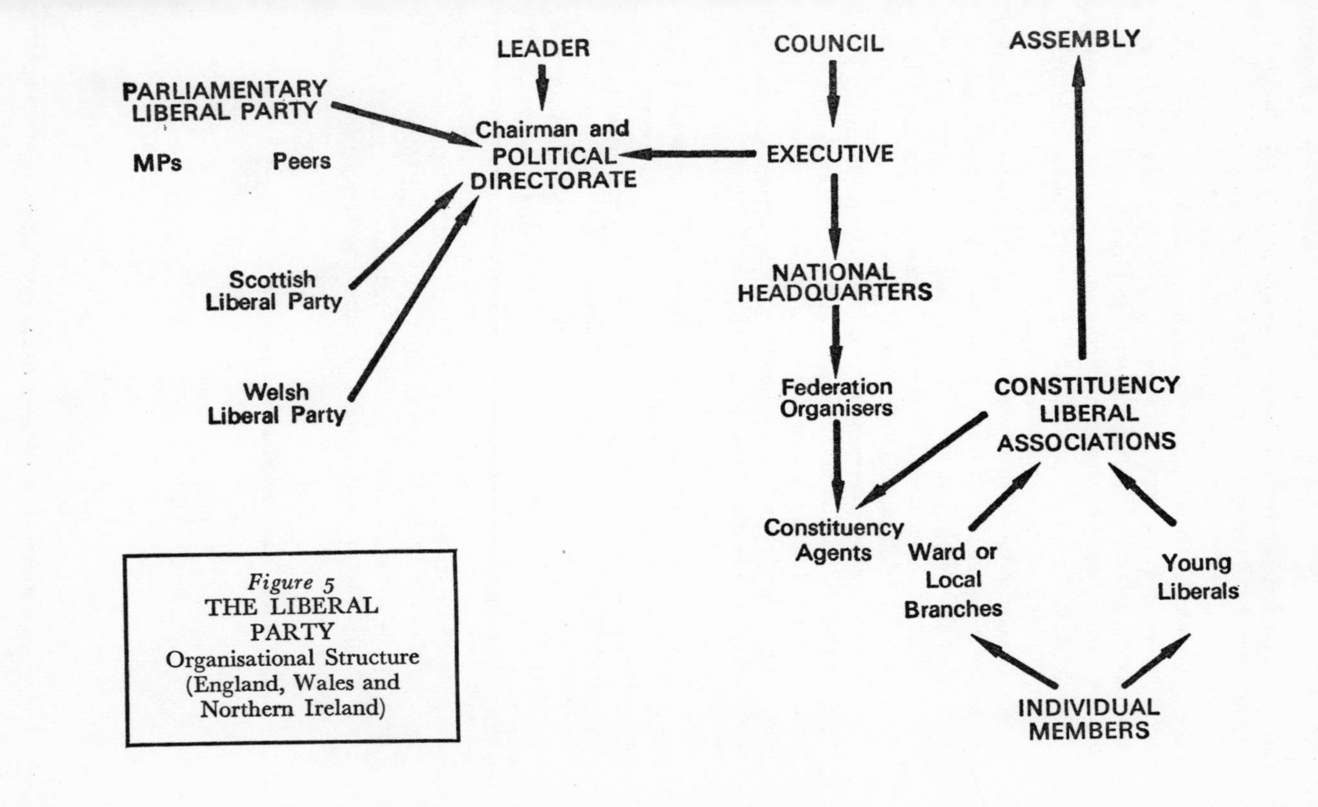

Figure 5
THE LIBERAL PARTY
Organisational Structure
(England, Wales and Northern Ireland)

revival and has enjoyed a number of electoral successes, though in 1966 it could still boast of no more than a dozen MPs.

The leader of the party is elected by the Liberal MPs and, as in the other parties, is recognized as leader of the whole party. The most recent occasion was in January 1967, when Jeremy Thorpe was elected, following the resignation of Jo Grimond.

The extra-Parliamentary organization of the party is known as the Liberal Party Organization and it is run according to a constitution adopted in 1936, and revised in 1967.

At its apex is the Liberal Assembly, or party conference, which meets once a year and to which each constituency Liberal association sends delegates. The size of the Assembly has fluctuated with the fortunes of the Liberal Party but in recent years there have been about 800 delegates. The Assembly elects by ballot the officers of the party and its representatives on the Liberal Council. This body, with between 100 and 200 members, meets four times a year and is responsible for policy decisions between meetings of the Assembly. Subordinate to the council is the executive committee, of some forty to fifty members, which effectively controls the party headquarters and bureaucracy.

To co-ordinate the work of the Parliamentary Party with that of the party organization in England, and also with the autonomous Liberal organizations in Wales and Scotland, a new position was instituted in 1967—that of party chairman. The chairman is appointed by the leader, and he works in conjunction with the political directorate, which is composed of representatives of all the leading organs of the party.

The last Liberal government, led successively by Campbell-Bannerman and Asquith, held office from 1910 to 1916. Liberals took part in the Lloyd George coalition government from 1916 to 1922, briefly in the Ramsay MacDonald national government from 1931 to 1932 and in the Churchill coalition government from 1939 to 1945.

Table 9—Liberal Party candidates since 1945

Year	*Candidates*	*Elected*
1945	306	12
1950	475	9
1951	109	6
1955	110	6
1959	216	6
1964	365	9
1966	311	12

Average vote per candidate in 1966: 16·3%

The membership of the Liberal Party at the beginning of 1964 was 350,000. Since then there has been no census of party members, but it is likely that the numbers have fallen.

The number of candidates that have been put in the field by the Liberal Party in post-war elections has fluctuated widely.

Minor parties

The *Communist Party* of Great Britain, founded in 1920, is the most prominent of the minor parties with a national following. It claimed a membership of 34,568 in June 1963, with some 1,200 branches. It employs about one hundred people either in its London headquarters at King Street near Covent Garden or on organizational work throughout the country. Communist MPs were elected to Parliament in 1922, 1924, 1935 and 1945, but the party has been without Parliamentary representation since 1950.

Table 10—Communist Party candidates since 1945

Year	*Candidates*	*Elected*
1945	21	2
1950	100	0
1951	10	0
1955	17	0
1959	18	0
1964	36	0
1966	57	0

Average vote per candidate in 1966: 3·0%

The *Welsh Nationalist Party* (or Plaid Cymru), with headquarters in Cardiff, has contested a majority of the Welsh constituencies in the last three general elections. It won its first Parliamentary contest ever in a by-election at Carmarthen in July 1966. Its membership in November 1966 was just over 20,000, organized in 242 branches. Founded in 1925, its programme is self-government for Wales. Its greatest strength lies in the Welsh-speaking areas of north and west Wales.

Table 11—Plaid Cymru candidates since 1945

Year	*Candidates*	*Elected*
1945	8	0
1950	7	0
1951	4	0
1955	11	0
1959	20	0
1964	23	0
1966	19	0

Average vote per candidate in 1966: 8·7%

The *Scottish National Party*, whose headquarters are in Glasgow, was founded in 1928 with the aim of securing self-government for Scotland. Its first Parliamentary seat, Motherwell, won at a by-election in April 1945, was lost three months later in the 1945 general election. In November 1967 its second by-election victory was recorded, at Hamilton. Its strength has been increasing in recent years, and in the 1966 general election it polled more votes than any other minor party. Its membership in June 1966 was 25,000, organized in over 250 branches.

Table 12—Scottish National Party candidates since 1945

Year	*Candidates*	*Elected*
1945	8	0
1950	4	0
1951	1	0
1955	2	0
1959	5	0
1964	15	0
1966	23	0

Average vote per candidate in 1966: 14·1%

The *Sinn Fein*, the political branch of the now disbanded terrorist organization, the Irish Republican Army, was founded during the First World War. In the 1918 general election it won sixty-nine out of the 103 Irish seats which it contested. Since the establishment of Northern Ireland, it won one Parliamentary constituency in 1922 and 1923 and then seemed to have passed into history. In 1955 and 1959 it reappeared, however, and contested all twelve seats in Northern Ireland mostly nominating convicted terrorists as its candidates. Two were elected in 1955 but were later disqualified as felons (see p. 66, below). In 1964 and 1966 no Sinn Fein candidates were nominated, but several former Sinn Feiners stood under the label "Republican." They drew most of their support from strongly Roman Catholic areas.

Various other *Irish Nationalist* candidates have contested Northern Irish seats, and from 1922 to 1955 between one and three constituencies were continuously represented by Irish Nationalist Members, who usually refused to take their seats in the House of Commons. In 1966 a Republican Labour Member was elected by the Belfast West constituency—he *did*, however, take his seat in the House.

Other parties

In addition to the recognized minor parties, there are many other "fringe" groups which put up Parliamentary candidates from time to time. Many of these have a purely ephemeral existence; few have more than a handful of members, and none, except the ILP, has ever come anywhere near to winning even one seat in the House of Commons. Most of these fringe groups are either on the left of the Labour Party or on the right of the Conservatives—few of them adopt a centre position.

The oldest of these parties is the *Independent Labour Party* (ILP), formed in 1893 and one of the founding bodies which established the Labour Party in 1900. It remained affiliated to the Labour Party until 1932 and, at its peak in 1929, had thirty-seven Members of Parliament. After 1932 its membership declined to a few hundred and the only area in which it retained much support was in Glasgow, where it continued to be represented in Parliament until 1950. The ILP's policy is strongly internationalist and, though anti-Communist, it is well to the left of the Labour Party. It now has only a tiny following.

Another left-wing party with a long history is the *Socialist Party of Great Britain* (SPGB), founded in 1904. The *Socialist Labour League* is now the leading Trotskyist organization, and the *Communist Anti-Revisionists* are a pro-Chinese breakaway group from the Communist Party. The *Radical Alliance*, founded in 1965, is opposed to the Labour Government's foreign policy.

On the right wing are several groups which put forward more or less blatantly racialist platforms. The best known of these is probably the *Union Movement* of Sir Oswald Mosley, founded in 1948 as the successor to his pre-war British Union of Fascists. The *British National Party*, which put up several candidates in 1964 and 1966 in constituencies with many immigrant voters, has had rather more success at the polls, perhaps because it has advanced a less extremist programme.[8]

A wide variety of *Independent* candidates, often wearing bizarre labels, offer themselves at each general election and at occasional by-elections. Few independent candidates poll more than a few hundred votes, except when one or other of the two major parties does not contest the constituency (a rare event). The only independents who have been elected since 1945 have been returned with the, more or less, open support of the Conservative Party. Thus, Sir David Robertson, a former Conservative MP for the same constituency, was elected for Caithness and Sutherland in 1959 and

[8] For more detailed information about very small parties see George Thayer, *The British Political Fringe* (London, Blond, 1965). See also the chapter on "The Fringe Left," in Gerald Kaufman (ed.), *The Left* (London, Blond, 1967).

Mr G. Forrest, who later took the Conservative whip, was elected for Mid-Ulster in a by-election in 1956. The only other Members to be elected since 1945 without being official party nominees were the Speakers of the House of Commons who, in 1950, 1955 and 1966, were elected without opposition from the political parties in the constituencies which they had formerly represented as Conservative or Labour MPs.

6. Political Parties—Local

THE NATIONAL ORGANIZATIONS OF THE POLITICAL PARTIES MONOPOLIZE publicity in the Press and on radio and television, but it is the local branches with which the voter is likely to come into contact.

Both the Conservative and Labour parties have branches in each of the 630 constituencies (although the Labour Party may have no effective organization in a few of the county constituencies in Northern Ireland). The Liberal Party's coverage is less comprehensive, but in October 1966 it had some sort of organization in 419 constituencies, compared with 475 three years earlier.

A constituency party (or association as it is called by Conservatives and Liberals) is not normally the nearest the parties get to the grass roots. Local branches are organized at ward level in towns and cities and in villages and small towns in country areas. Here, however, the two main parties' coverage is less complete. In hopeless constituencies in industrial towns, and especially in mining areas, there are some constituencies where the Conservative ward organization is rudimentary or non-existent. In the counties, too, there are many villages and small towns without any Labour organization. Liberal organization below constituency level is extremely patchy. In a very few constituencies they match or even better the coverage of the larger parties. In probably a majority of constituencies, however, there is no Liberal organization below constituency level.

It is the ward or local party, at least in the Conservative and Labour parties, which is the basic level of party organization. The ward party is the actual unit to which party members belong; it is responsible for recruiting new members and collecting subscriptions and for the great majority of party members it is the only organ of the party with which they have any contact.

The typical ward or village party meets every month, usually in the house of one of its members, sometimes in a hired school room or village hall, occasionally on party premises. The number of members varies enormously, both according to the size of the electorate in the area covered (which will range from a tiny village to a large ward in a city with anything up to fifteen to twenty thousand electors) and the strength of the party in that area. In practice, the membership is unlikely to be less than half a dozen nor more than 1,500. The great majority of members do no more than pay their subscriptions to the party, when they are called on at their homes. The attendance at most ward or local party meetings is likely to range between six and forty, averaging between 5 and 20 per cent of the members in most towns, though in country areas the percentage attendance is likely to be considerably higher.

The minimum subscription to each of the parties is small—very small when compared to the subscriptions paid to political parties in most other countries. The Labour Party's minimum subscription is 12s. a year (raised from 6s. in 1965); neither the Conservatives nor the Liberals have an official minimum subscription, and many of their rank-and-file members pay as little as 5s. or even less. The subscription to the Conservative and Liberal parties is normally collected by an annual visit to the member's home. In most areas the Labour Party made arrangements, in the past, for the monthly or even weekly collection of smaller amounts. With the fall in the value of money, however, such arrangements are now an exception. Most Labour members now subscribe quarterly or half-yearly, while an increasing proportion make a single annual payment. The collection of subscriptions is mainly carried out on a voluntary basis by keen party members, though all three parties resort in many areas to paid collectors who may also receive a percentage of the amount that they collect. There is a great deal of inefficiency in the machinery for collecting subscriptions and it is apparent that each party loses a substantial amount each year because of this. Many branches with a potentially larger membership refrain from attempting to recruit new members because of a lack of volunteers to act as collectors.

The minority of party members who attend the monthly meeting of the party often find only a small part of its agenda is devoted to political matters. Many ward meetings, particularly in the Labour Party, have a speaker to address them on a subject of national importance and there may be a resolution to discuss on the social services or a foreign policy issue. It is equally likely, however, that the agenda will consist almost exclusively of administrative matters, particularly those concerned with fund raising. It is not unusual for a local party to spend more time discussing who is to look after the sweet stall at the party's jumble sale than it devotes to considering possible resolutions for the annual conference of the party. It follows from this that local party branches are as much social as political affairs and the sense of comradeship at this, the lowest level of party politics, is strong.

In areas in which parties are weak, local and ward parties often have an ephemeral existence depending for their existence primarily on the enthusiasm of one or two members who provide the impetus for the others. A loss of interest on the part of one or two individuals, or their removal from the neighbourhood, may cause the branch to collapse altogether and go out of existence. Then, after an interval of perhaps several years, an enthusiastic newcomer will start things up again and with the aid of old and unreliable records will call on long dormant members and try to rekindle their interest.

Even in areas in which a party is strong its local branches will not necessarily be flourishing. The absence of challenge from the other side may breed apathy and the party organization, however strong on paper, may be sickly and lethargic. It is in marginal constituencies, where there is a constant electoral challenge, that the local parties on both sides are most likely to be large and active organisations.

There is a wide variation in the nature and circumstances of local branches. Differences within each of the three main parties are often greater than those between them. At this, the lowest level of organization, the procedures and functions of branches of all political parties are very similar, so much so that there is no need here to distinguish between them. The only consistent difference is that there is less political discussion in Conservative than in Labour or Liberal branches, but even to this general rule there are manifold exceptions.

Depending on its strength and its circumstances, a local branch will have a number of officials. The minimum is normally a chairman, honorary secretary, and honorary treasurer, though in very small branches even these offices might be doubled up. There are normally also one or more vice-chairmen and a number of other functional offices, of which canvassing officer, social secretary, membership officer, literature secretary, and raffle officer or tote organizer are most common. There may also be an assistant secretary and, in the case of the larger and more active branches, an executive committee whose membership would include most or all of the officers listed listed above.

The most active members of the branch will also be delegates to the managing body of the constituency party, known as the Executive Council in the Conservative Party, the General Management Committee (GMC) in the Labour Party and the Executive Committee in the Liberal Party.

It is this body which contains the hard core of militants, usually of between twenty and one hundred attending members (though the nominal membership may be higher), who keep the wheels of the party organization turning throughout the country. At this level there is a notable difference between the parties. The managing body of a Conservative or Liberal constituency association will contain, in addition to representatives of ward and local branches, delegates from women's organizations and of the Young Conservatives and Young Liberals respectively. A Labour GMC similarly contains representatives from wards, Young Socialists and women's sections but will also include delegates from affiliated organizations—trade unions, co-operative organizations and, perhaps, a local Fabian Society. For every individual member of the Labour Party there are five affiliated members and the nominal membership of a great many GMCs is made up predominantly of the delegates from affiliated bodies. Many of these are inactive, and it is very rare for there to be a majority of delegates of affiliated organizations among those actually attending. On special occasions, such as the selection of a Parliamentary candidate, however, it sometimes happens that a meeting of a GMC is crowded out by an influx of unfamiliar delegates who may never appear again.

The governing bodies of constituency parties are important and influential organizations. They are responsible for fighting elections, both Parliamentary and local government, and for all practical purposes are the voice of the national party within their own areas.

Most of them meet monthly and, as in the case of local branches, much of their time is devoted to discussing financial and administrative matters. Constituency Labour parties, particularly those which are strongly left wing, frequently pass resolutions of a political nature, which are sent to Transport House for consideration by the National Executive Committee. Protests at the actions or omissions of the party leadership or of Transport House officials are also frequently registered, with little apparent effect. Liberal and Conservative associations make their views known to their respective head offices with far less frequency.

Constituency parties elect delegates to the annual party conference, who may or may not be instructed on how to cast their votes on the most controversial issues to be debated at the conference. It is usual for each constituency party to send one resolution to the annual conference, though here again the right is more often asserted by Labour parties than by Liberal or Conservative associations. The most important *political* act of constituency parties is undoubtedly, however, the selection of Parliamentary candidates. This is discussed in detail in Chapter 7.

The ward and local parties are, in most respects, definitely subordinate to the constituency parties. Each constituency party has a full panoply of officers—chairman, vice-chairman, honorary treasurer, secretary, assistant secretary, and numerous other people designated to do specific tasks. In the Conservative and Labour parties, sub-committees of the constituency party's governing body, known respectively as the finance and general purposes committee (Conservative) and the executive committee (Labour) are responsible for the day-to-day running of the constituency party. Conservative constituency organizations normally have several other standing sub-committees and make provision for both Young Conservatives and women members to be largely represented on all organs of the party.

The principal function of constituency parties is to maintain an electoral organization in a constant state of readiness. Constituency parties able to maintain a full-time agent find this a much more manageable task. The Conservatives are much better placed in this respect. At the time of the 1966 general election they employed 499 full-time agents who assumed responsibility for 537 constituencies. At the same time the Labour Party had 202 agents in the field and the Liberals sixty. The Conservative and Labour figures have remained fairly constant for about a decade, but the number of Liberal agents has fluctuated violently. There were nearly eighty in 1964, but by November 1966—eight months after the 1966 election—the number had fallen to thirty.

Most agents earn between £800 and £1,500 a year, the rate of pay in the Conservative Party being higher than in the Labour and Liberal parties. It is the two latter, however, that experience the greatest difficulty in paying their agents' salaries, and many Labour and Liberal agents spend a great deal more of their time running money-raising schemes, the main purpose of which is to meet their own salaries. They then have little time left over for organizing work. The headquarters of the Conservative and Labour parties have a limited amount of money at their disposal to help constituency parties to employ agents. Their money is channelled into the marginal constituencies: other constituency parties wishing to employ an agent are expected to pay their own way.

Full-time agents normally act as secretaries to the constituency parties which employ them.

The activities of constituency parties between elections are varied. Among the most important are to keep the name and activities of its Member of Parliament or prospective Parliamentary candidate continually in the public eye. (Candidates are invariably known as *prospective* candidates in the period until the general election campaign begins. Otherwise money spent on the candidate's activities between elections might be legally chargeable to his election expenses, which are restricted by law. See Chapter 14, below.)

The traditional method of doing this is the public meeting. With the spread of television and other mass media interest in public meetings has declined in the post-war period, though there is some recent evidence that it is now increasing. Nevertheless, few constituency parties in borough constituencies now organize more than four public meetings a year and many do far less. The meetings, normally addressed by the MP or prospective candidate and two or three other speakers, are publicized through posters, local newspaper advertisements and by the delivery of leaflets. When one of the speakers is a nationally known figure considerable extra effort may be put into planning the meeting. In some areas a great deal of apathy is encountered and the hard core of active party members will make up by far the greater part of the audience. In other areas good attendances are obtained, and lively meetings may be expected if "the opposition" turns up to have its say. It seems likely that many constituency parties take an unduly defeatist view of the public demand for meetings and that if they took the trouble to organize them well, to obtain competent and varied speakers and to publicize them widely and in good time, they would get better audiences than they imagine.

Most Members of Parliament and some prospective candidates hold regular "surgeries" to which their constituents may come with their personal problems. Pensions and housing are the subjects which recur most frequently, but an extremely wide range of problems are referred to MPs for their help and advice. Often it is a question of referring the constituent to the proper authority—the Ministry of Social Security, the housing department of the local council or the public health authority. Sometimes, however, a Member can be of direct assistance by taking up a case personally with a Minister or asking a question in Parliament. This "welfare work" of MPs is one of their most important activities and it consumes an increasing proportion of their time and energies. In so far as Members of Parliament have a personal vote, it is more likely to be built up laboriously over the years through diligent application to the personal problems of constituents than by any more flamboyant action or gesture.

The agent or secretary will always be on the look out for other ways of pushing his MP or prospective candidate into the limelight. If a local organization—a church or youth club, a dramatic society, a rotary club or any one of a hundred others—wants somebody to open a bazaar, distribute prizes or make a speech (quite often on a non-political subject) he has just the man for the job. The value of such assignments for prospective candidates lies at least as much in the report which will follow in the local newspaper as in the activity itself.

Most constituency parties organize membership drives from time to time in which their members call from house to house, usually in what are regarded as favourable areas, trying to persuade people to join. Little time is normally wasted on attempting to convert "hostile" elements, but anyone who shows interest will be carefully fostered. In such cases a further visit by the Parliamentary candidate or party secretary may well be arranged.

A different sort of canvassing is designed to provide a reliable record of voting intentions of the electorate. The purpose is to obtain a "marked register," so that the party has a good idea of where its support lies when the election is due. Copies of the election register are cut up and stuck on hard boards—and party members are asked to mark "F," "A" or "D" against the name of each voter after calling at their houses. These abbreviations stand for "for," "against" and "doubtful." The proceedings at each house are crisp and seldom long prolonged. Most canvassers adopt an apologetic stance and mumble something along these lines: "Good evening, Mrs Jones? I'm calling on behalf of the... Party. We wonder whether we can rely on your support at the next election."

The response to this enquiry is varied, but rudeness is extremely rare. "Yes, you can depend on us" or "We always vote on the day" are likely rejoinders from party supporters. "I'm afraid we're on the other side" or "You've called at the wrong house, old chap" are the limits to the hostility which the average canvasser can expect to encounter. There *are* voters who will say: "If I had a hundred votes I wouldn't give one to your lot" or even "If you come this way again I'll set my dog on you," but they are few and far between.

A subsidiary object of house-to-house canvassing is to discover invalids and other people who would be eligible for postal votes, so that they may be helped to claim them. Relatively few voters take this initiative themselves, without prompting from their party. The party which organizes the largest number of postal votes in a marginal constituency may find that this has made all the difference between victory and defeat. There is no doubt that the Conservatives are more alive than the other parties to the need to build up a large postal vote and that they have hitherto enjoyed much greater success in this sphere.

Elections to local authorities absorb a great deal of the time and money of many constituency parties. Outside London they take place every year in May, with county council elections every three years in April. In London the local authority elections are also once every three years. Local elections help parties to keep their electoral organization in a state of readiness for the general election and the canvassing results help the party to maintain an up-to-date "marked register."

It can happen, however, that excessive preoccupation with local government matters can hinder a constituency party's ability to fight an effective general election campaign. The more able members may have become aldermen or councillors and may devote so much time to council affairs that they have little to spare for the party. If the party controls the town council, unpopular decisions by the council, such as raising council house rents, may adversely affect the party's electoral appeal at a Parliamentary election.

The ownership or tenancy of premises can have a similarly two-edged effect on a constituency party. Parties employing a full-time agent obviously need premises to provide an office in which he can work and to store the party records. It is a great advantage, too, to have a hall in which to hold meetings and to use as committee rooms at election time. And a permanent headquarters acts as a focus for a wide variety of party activities. There is danger, however, that if the premises are used extensively for social activities the political work of the party will suffer. In such circumstances the premises may be a heavy drain on the party's funds without producing any equivalent benefit to its electoral prospects.

Money raising is a perennial problem for constituency parties. Few of them derive sufficient income from subscriptions and donations to meet even their most essential commitments. The gap is met in nine cases out of ten by appeals to the gambling instinct. There are a few parties, where the Nonconformist conscience is strong, which succeed in rising above such expedients. But the Colne Valley Labour Party, which raises £500 a year through a gift day, run along the lines of a church harvest festival, is all but unique. In all three major parties it is normally the raffle or whist drive, the bingo session, the football pool or tote scheme which keeps the local branches solvent. The income which constituency parties derive from such sources varies from a few pounds to about £10,000 per annum. The latter amount is rarely reached but a large number of parties make between £500 and £2,000 out of their fund-raising schemes.

There is no published information about the funds of constituency parties, but seventy different parties sent their balance sheets for the year 1962–63 to the present author in response to an enquiry which he made while compiling this book. This enquiry revealed an average income for Conservative associations of £3,100, for Labour parties of £2,000 and for Liberal associations of £690. It seems likely that the figure for the income of Conservative associations revealed by this sample is rather on the low side but the figures for the Labour and Liberal parties were probably about right. In the four years since then it would be realistic to assume that the average income of constituency parties would have grown by about 10 per cent.

An indication of the main sources of income and expenditure of a moderately prosperous constituency party is given by the following imaginary income and expenditure account:

Expenditure	£	*Income*	£
Agent's salary	1,000	Subscriptions	450
Clerical help	350	Football competition	1,400
Agent's expenses	200	Dances	175
Rent and office charges	200	Bazaar	180
Postage, telephone	150	Derby draw	200
Stationery	100	Financial appeal	130
Publications	75	Miscellaneous	65
Subscription to head office	100		
Depreciation of equipment	50		
Local elections	125		
General election fighting fund	170		
Miscellaneous	80		
Total	2,600	Total	2,600

Each of the parties has youth organizations which are made up of branches formed on a constituency basis or to cover a smaller area within a constituency. The branches are represented on the governing bodies of constituency parties.

The Young Conservatives, with rather over 100,000 members in 1,400 branches, are much the largest and most powerful of the three organizations. Many of the branches are primarily social organizations but Young Conservatives, particularly in suburban areas, provide much of the manpower for canvassing teams and other electoral activities. There is no doubt that they represent a valuable asset to the Conservative Party.

The Labour Party Young Socialists have about 18,000 members in 571 branches. More political than their Conservative counterparts, they often embarrass the Labour Party by embracing policies well to the left of the leadership. Many branches play an important part in the party organization, particularly at election times, but overall the Young Socialists have undoubtedly proved less of an asset to their party than have the Young Conservatives to theirs.

The Young Liberals also have some 18,000 members in about 415 branches.[1] Their contribution to the work of the Liberal Party is very comparable to that of the Young Socialists to Labour.

[1] The membership figures for the three youth organizations are as supplied by the respective Party headquarters in October, 1966.

7. Candidates

Who is Eligible

NO SPECIAL QUALIFICATIONS WHATEVER ARE LEGALLY REQUIRED OF Parliamentary candidates; the only positive requirements are those which also apply to voters—that is, to be a British or Commonwealth subject or a citizen of the Republic of Ireland, and to have reached the age of twenty-one. It is not even necessary to be on the election register, and "Y" voters may be candidates before they have qualified to vote providing they have passed their twenty-first birthday.

There are, however, a number of disqualifications which together exclude a considerable number of people from being elected. People in the following categories are disqualified:

Peers. English and Scottish peers, unless they have renounced their peerage during their lifetime. Irish peers are not disqualified.

Clergy. Clergy of the Church of England or the Church of Ireland, ministers of the Church of Scotland and Roman Catholic priests. Clergy of the Church of Wales and non-conformist ministers are *not* disqualified.

Aliens, but those who have acquired British citizenship through naturalization are eligible, as are citizens of Commonwealth countries.

Members of Legislatures outside the Commonwealth. These would normally be excluded as aliens, but the effect of this provision is to disqualify the exceptional case of people with dual nationality, and members of the Seanad and Dáil of the Republic of Ireland.

Certified Lunatics.

Bankrupts. Undischarged bankrupts are disqualified from six months after the date of adjudication and remain so until either the bankruptcy is annulled or a grant of discharge is awarded, accompanied by a certificate that the bankruptcy was not due to misconduct.

Felons. Following conviction, felons are disqualified and remain so until they have served their sentence or received a free pardon.

Corrupt and illegal practices at elections. Persons convicted of such practices may be disqualified for varying periods (see Appendix 6).

Much the largest number of people disqualified from membership of the House of Commons, however, are those who hold *offices of profit under the Crown.* This includes sheriffs, judges, civil servants and a very wide and varied list of office-holders, many of whom receive only nominal remuneration for their services.

Before 1957 there was an immense degree of confusion as to what actually constituted an office of profit. Members elected to the House of Commons who performed public service, such as membership of Rent Tribunals, found to their dismay and astonishment that they were disqualified from membership of the House and liable to pay extremely high monetary penalties (£500 per day) for sitting and voting in the House. Ten members found themselves in this position between 1945 and 1955, and in nine cases the House passed emergency legislation to validate their position. In the other case, Mr C. Beattie, the Member for Mid-Ulster in 1955, had to vacate his seat and a by-election was held to replace him.

The confusion which existed before 1957 was due to the fact that the different disqualifying offices had resulted from over one hundred Acts of Parliament enacted over a period of 250 years and there was no list of these offices to which would-be candidates could refer to see whether they were disqualified. The position was clarified, however, by the 1957 House of Commons Disqualification Act which contained two schedules, one listing specific offices which do disqualify, the other listing those which do not.

It is highly advisable for all would-be candidates to study these lists before accepting nomination—as there is now little excuse for candidates who transgress through ignorance.

It should perhaps be added that, though civil servants are disqualified from membership of the House of Commons, schoolteachers, employees of nationalized industries and local government employees are all eligible.

Armed forces. The final category of people disqualified from membership of Parliament are members of the armed forces. It had, however, been normal for a serviceman seeking nomination to be discharged. In 1962, an ingenious soldier, Malcolm Thompson, who had been refused a discharge in order to enrol as a university student, offered himself as an independent candidate at a by-election at Middlesbrough West and consequently secured his demobilization. Later the same year twelve more servicemen followed his example, several of them discovering that they did not even have to be nominated (and thus have to pay a deposit of £150) to secure their discharge; it was sufficient just to apply for nomination papers.

By the end of the year, when further by-elections were expected at Colne Valley and Rotherham, it appeared that the trickle of servicemen using this means to obtain a cheap and easy discharge was threatening to become a flood. No less than 174 requests were received for nomination papers at Colne Valley and 493 at Rotherham. A Select Committee of the House of Commons reported that the problem was a most complex one and that it would take much care and thought to devise a permanent solution. As a temporary expedient, to meet the need to proceed with the by-elections already pending, it recommended the appointment of a small advisory committee which would vet applications by servicemen wishing to be candidates and would advise the appropriate service Ministers whether to grant a discharge.[1]

This recommendation was approved by the House of Commons in February 1963 and a committee consisting of two Queen's Counsel and six former MPs was appointed by the Home Secretary. Its function was to examine the application of each would-be candidate (who would normally be personally interviewed by the committee) and decide whether he had genuine Parliamentary ambitions. The unsatisfactory nature of this expedient was soon apparent. Of the twenty-six servicemen who actually applied to the committee in connection with the Colne Valley and Rotherham by-elections only one was recommended for discharge. But as soon as he had secured his demobilization he announced that he had changed his mind and did not offer himself as candidate.

In June 1963 the Select Committee reported that it was still unable to suggest a permanent solution to the problem, and it recommended that the advisory committee should continue to function.[2] In the period up to October 1966 the committee interviewed fifty-two would-be candidates, of whom only four were recommended for release. The imposition of this stiff hurdle seems to have successfully staunched the flow of servicemen seeking discharge through this means. Only five applied to stand in the 1964 general election and one in 1966.

Although all the above categories disqualify from membership of the House of Commons, there is in practice no means of preventing a disqualified person presenting himself as a candidate. The responsibility of a returning officer in vetting a nomination is confined to

[1] See House of Commons Paper, no. 111, 6 February, 1963.
[2] See House of Commons Paper, no. 262, 27 June, 1963.

ascertaining that the nomination form has been properly filled in and signed by the requisite number of electors. He is not required to satisfy himself that the candidate is not a disqualified person.

In practice, no political party would normally agree to support a candidate known to be disqualified,[3] and few disqualified people would consent to nomination. Occasionally, however, such a candidate is nominated as a gesture. Thus in 1955 and 1959, as also on earlier occasions, several candidates serving prison sentences were nominated by Sinn Fein in Northern Ireland constituencies. In 1955 two of them were elected, Mr Thomas Mitchell for Mid-Ulster and Mr P. Clarke for Fermanagh and South Tyrone. In 1961 Mr Anthony Wedgwood Benn (the former Lord Stansgate) successfully contested, as the Labour candidate, a by-election in his constituency of Bristol South-East, although disqualified at that time as a peer.

In the event of a disqualified person being elected, it is open to his defeated opponent to apply to the High Court to have his election declared void. When this has occurred, the committee has held that if the facts leading to the disqualification had been generally known to the electors, those who have voted for the disqualified candidate should be deemed to have thrown their votes away, and the runner-up has been declared elected in his place. This indeed happened in the cases of both Mr Clarke and Mr Wedgwood Benn. In the case of Mr Mitchell, however, the defeated candidate did not petition the High Court, but the seat was declared vacant by a resolution of the House of Commons. In the ensuing by-election Mr Mitchell was again elected, and on this occasion his Ulster Unionist opponent, Mr C. Beattie, secured the seat by virtue of an election petition. But his triumph was short-lived, as mentioned on page 64, he was found to hold an office of profit and had to vacate the seat. So in this minor comedy of errors it took one general election, an election petition and two by-elections to secure an eligible Member for Mid-Ulster in the 1955 Parliament.

Where a disqualified person has been elected, without the facts leading to the disqualification being generally known to the electorate, the runner-up is not elected in his place, but a by-election is held to find a successor. This occurred in Belfast West in 1950, when the Rev J. G. MacManaway, a clergyman of the Church of Ireland, was elected, and it was not established until later that he was disqualified.

[3] Though the Rev. R. C. Gaul, a clergyman of the Church of England, was nominated as a Liberal candidate at Louth in 1951 and at Grantham in 1955.

How Candidates are Chosen

The procedures of the three main political parties for selecting candidates differ in a number of important details, but are basically similar. In each case the selection is the responsibility of the local constituency party and the influence of the party headquarters is relatively minor.

A pamphlet published by the Conservative Central Office for the guidance of local associations states: "Subject to certain simple party rules each association has complete freedom to select the man or woman of its choice." There are well-established procedures within the Conservative Party which limit, however, the degree of local variation in methods of selection.

The executive council of a Conservative association wishing to select a new candidate appoints a selection committee, usually of about six members, who would be amongst the most influential and senior members of the association. The chairman of the association is invariably included unless, which is not infrequently the case, he has ambitions to be selected himself. The purpose of the selection committee is to consider all the possible aspirants for the candidature and reduce them to a small number from which the executive council may make its choice.

The constituency chairman is expected to obtain from the Central Office a list of names of suitable people, together with biographical details. One of the vice-chairmen of the National Union, assisted by the standing advisory committee on candidates, is responsible for maintaining an official list of approved potential candidates from among whom a number of names would be sent. Any member of the Conservative Party may apply to be included on the official list, and he is then interviewed by the vice-chairman or by members of the standing advisory committee, and, if approved, his name is added to the list.

Together with the names obtained from Central Office, the selection committee considers any members of the constituency association who have expressed an interest in the candidature and also the names of Conservatives who may have written asking to be considered. If it is a safe Conservative seat there may be a large number of these and it is not uncommon for a selection committee to have over a hundred names from which to choose.

The selection committee quickly whittle this number down to about seven or eight, and in the case of a safe seat few of the applicants would have much chance of surviving to this stage unless they were nationally known figures, were obviously extremely well qualified or were personally known to a member of the selection committee.

The seven or eight people chosen are invited to attend to be interviewed by the selection committee which then chooses normally two or three names from whom the executive council may make its final choice. Occasionally, however, when the selection committee decide, in the words of the Central Office pamphlet, that "a candidate is available whose record is so distinguished and whose qualifications are so outstanding that his adoption is practically a foregone conclusion" only one name is put forward to the executive council.

Before this stage is reached the names of any of the surviving nominees who are not included on the approved Central Office list are submitted to the standing advisory committee for endorsement. If endorsement is refused and the constituency proceeds to select a nominee in spite of this, he is not regarded as an official party candidate at the ensuing election. Cases of an association selecting a candidate who has not been previously approved, are, however, extremely rare.

The nominees put forward by the selection committee attend a selection conference of the executive council. Each makes a short speech (normally limited to a period varying between ten and thirty minutes) and answers questions put to him from the floor. A secret ballot is then held to choose who will be the candidate. There is no provision in the party rules as to the conduct of this ballot. It is possible for the nominee leading on the first ballot to be chosen forthwith, even though only a minority may have voted for him. It is far more usual, however, for an exhaustive ballot to be held, with the bottom candidate falling out if no overall majority is obtained on the first ballot.

The executive council's choice is submitted for approval to a general meeting of the whole association. This is normally a formality, but there have been occasions in which the executive council's choice has been challenged at this stage and another name substituted.

Money nowadays plays no significant part in the selection of Conservative candidates. This has not always been so. Up till 1948 it was very common for Conservative candidates to defray the whole of their election expenses and in addition to pay a large annual subscription to the constituency association. Consequently wealth was a prerequisite for potential Conservative Members, with very few exceptions.

The shock of defeat in 1945, however, led to a comprehensive reappraisal of the organization of the Conservative Party following the report of a committee presided over by Sir David Maxwell Fyfe (who later became Lord Kilmuir). Its recommendations, which were accepted by the party, have fundamentally altered the financial relationship between Conservative MPs and candidates and their constituency associations. Under the new rules a Conservative candidate is precluded from making any contribution whatever towards the election expenses, other than his personal expenses. The maximum contribution which he may make to his association is £25 a year as a candidate, and £50 a year as an MP. In no circumstances, state the party rules, may the payment of a subscription be made a condition of adoption.

There can be no doubt that the new rules are substantially adhered to, and the result has been that a large number of Conservative candidates without private means have been selected in the period since 1948. Whilst wealth is no handicap in the Conservative Party and rich men are often selected as candidates, money no longer plays a direct part in their selection.

The Labour Party's selection procedure is laid down in more detail in the party rules, and it is complicated by the existence of two classes of membership, individual and affiliated (principally trade unions). When a constituency party decides to select a candidate, its executive committee first consults with the regional organizer of the party to agree a timetable for the selection. The regional organizer is the representative of Transport House and it is his responsibility to ensure that the selection takes place according to the party rules. When the timetable has been approved by the general management committee of the constituency party, the secretary writes to each local or ward party or affiliated organization inviting them to make a nomination before a certain date, normally a minimum period of one month being allowed for this.

No person may be considered for selection unless he or she has been nominated by a local party or affiliated organization. There is no provision in the Labour Party for members to nominate themselves, though if a member has good personal contact with organizations with the right to nominate it is often not difficult for him to obtain a nomination.

Like the Conservative Central Office, Transport House maintains a list of possible Parliamentary candidates. It is in two parts: List A contains the names of individuals nominated by trade unions and in respect of whom the appropriate trade union is prepared to assume financial responsibility for the candidature. List B consists of persons nominated by constituency Labour parties and for whom no financial responsibility has been assumed.

The executive committee of a constituency party may ask for copies of either list for its own reference or to circulate to affiliated organizations, but there is no compulsion on them to do so, and frequently, particularly in the case of safe Labour seats, they make no effort to obtain the lists. There is little point in local parties in safe Conservative areas consulting list A, as trade unions are rarely willing to sponsor candidates who have no prospect of being elected. The more hopeless the seat, however, the more likely is a party to make use of list B and to write to perhaps a large number of the people included, asking them to accept nomination.

The number of nominations made varies enormously. In a "hopeless" rural constituency many miles from a large centre of population there may be as few as two or three. In a safe Labour-held seat in a borough, with many affiliated organizations, there is likely to be anything from ten to twenty-five nominations, and even the latter figure is often exceeded. Trade Union branches in safe Labour seats, particularly those of the larger unions, are likely to be approached by their union headquarters and asked to nominate a member of the union's parliamentary panel. These nominations must be accompanied by a letter from the general secretary of the union confirming that it will assume financial responsibility for the candidature. Trade union branches are also able to nominate unsponsored members of their unions whose standing is the same as that of nominees of ward or local Labour parties.

When the period for nomination has passed it is the responsibility of the executive committee (which itself has the right to make one nomination) to consider all the nominations received and to draw up a short list. If there are fewer than half a dozen nominations this is normally unnecessary, but this is a rare event, except in strong Tory areas. The executive committee may decide to interview all the nominees before drawing up a short list, or it may send them questionnaires to fill in. Often, however, it does neither.

The executive committee usually recommends a short list with from four to six names and this is reported to the general management committee for its approval. It is open to any member of the GMC to move the addition, substitution, or deletion of names and this occurs with considerable frequency, though more often than not amendments are voted down.

People on the approved short list are then invited to a selection conference of the GMC whose procedure is not unlike that of the executive council of a Conservative association, though an exhaustive ballot is prescribed in the party rules. The choice of the GMC does not have to be confirmed by a general meeting of members, as in the case of the Conservative Party, but his candidature must be endorsed by the national executive committee of the party.

It is paradoxical that financial considerations now play a greater part in the selection of Labour candidates than of Conservatives. The restrictions on individuals are similar—no Labour candidate may subscribe more than £50 a year to his constituency party, and this rule is seldom transgressed. In fact the average Labour candidate or MP undoubtedly subscribes less to his constituency party than his Conservative counterpart.

The monetary element in the Labour Party is represented by the system of trade union sponsorship of candidates, which goes back to the early days of the party when there was no individual membership and every candidature had to be sponsored by an official organization. Under the so-called Hastings Agreement, dating from the Labour Party conference at Hastings in 1933, a trade union is permitted to contribute up to 80 per cent of the election expenses incurred on behalf of its nominee and a maximum of £420 a year, or 60 per cent of the agent's salary, to the constituency party.

There is thus a strong temptation for hard-up constituency parties to choose a sponsored candidate, and this applies especially in safe Labour seats in industrial areas. Many constituency parties take a pride in choosing the best nominee available irrespective of financial considerations and many sponsored nominees are able and public-spirited men. There have, however, certainly been cases where more competent nominees have been passed over in favour of a mediocrity whose principal recommendation has been the income which his selection would ensure.

Under the party rules no mention of financial matters may be made at a selection conference and the regional organizer, who attends on behalf of Transport House, strictly enforces this rule. The significance of the distinction between trade union and local party nominees is likely, however, to be appreciated by at least the most alert of GMC members. But it is at the short-listing stage that sponsorship carries the greatest weight. For the executive committee of a constituency party is acutely aware of the difference that a sponsored candidate can make and, composed as it is of the dozen or so people with the greatest responsibility for the party's affairs, financial worries are likely to be very much on its mind. If an executive committee is determined to have a sponsored candidate it will recommend a short list made up entirely of those with financial backing, and there are fairly frequent examples of this occurring in safe Labour seats.

It is a difficult problem, as it is probably only the sponsorship system which enables a fair number of people from manual occupations to go straight from the workbench to the House of Commons and thus enable Parliament to contain a reasonable cross-section of the nation. If the system were abandoned it might result in the long run in the House being composed merely of people of the professional and middle classes, with a solid block of miners remaining as the only representative of manual workers. It is to be hoped, however, that one day the Labour Party will devise some method of supplanting the sponsorship system, without losing what has always been one of its most attractive features—the very wide range of background and occupation from which its candidates are drawn.

The Liberal Party's selection procedure is virtually identical to the Conservatives': the principal difference in practice is that there are nearly always far fewer nominees, and in many cases a Liberal association has the claims of only one contender to consider. In the relatively small number of cases where a candidate has to be found for a Liberal-held seat or one where there is a good chance of a Liberal victory the competition is far stronger, and the method of selection is very similar to that of the Conservative Party.

Unlike in the Conservative and Labour parties, there is no limit to the amount of money which Liberal candidates or MPs are allowed to contribute to their election expenses or donate to their constituency party. It is unlikely that more than a handful contribute more than the maximum imposed by both the Conservative and Labour parties.

The methods of selection of minor parties differ considerably from that of the major parties, principally because they have so few members. Decisions, normally taken in the larger parties by constituency associations, are more likely to be taken by the national committees of the smaller parties. Selection conferences of the type described above are the exception rather than the rule.

A few general points may be made about selection procedures of all parties. One is the small number of people involved in making the choice. The drawing up of the short list—a vital stage—is the responsibility in the Conservative Party of less than a dozen people and in the Labour Party of less than twenty. The final selection is seldom made by more than 200 people and most often by between fifty and 150. In the Liberal Party the numbers involved are even smaller.

The Selection Conference

The actual selection conference is the most dramatic stage in the selection process, and it is one that imposes considerable strain on the would-be candidates, as the author knows only too well from personal experience. It has been described by a former Tory MP, Nigel Nicolson, as "a gala occasion for the selectors; slow torture for the candidate."[4]

The nominees are asked to attend a conference lasting anything up to three or four hours, though most of the time they are cooped up in an ante-room with the other contenders while procedural matters are being discussed or one of their number is making his speech. There is a certain tactical advantage in being the last to speak (the order is normally decided by lot), but this is often offset by the tension of waiting until all your rivals have spoken. All one can hear of the proceedings are occasional muffled sounds of applause from which one imagines that one's rivals are making an extremely good impression. In fact the audience normally goes out of its way to encourage the nominees whose ordeal they can imagine, and are very free with their applause.

At last it is your turn. You are ushered into the conference, which as often as not is housed in a bleak Nonconformist church hall or school, but may occasionally be in the more regal surroundings of the council chamber of the town hall. Before you are perhaps eighty people, predominantly middle-aged, and you search eagerly for the encouragement of a familiar face, probably in vain.

You reach your seat on the platform, shake hands with the chairman, who announces that you are Mr X, whose biographical details have been circulated to all the delegates. You have fifteen minutes to speak and another fifteen minutes for questions. After fourteen minutes the chairman will sound a warning bell and after fifteen you will be stopped—if necessary in mid-sentence.

You stand up, try to show a confidence which you do not feel and launch into a well-prepared speech, which has been carefully timed in front of your bedroom mirror to last fourteen and a half minutes. In the event, you have either sat down after nine and a half minutes or are rudely cut short after fifteen minutes—less than a third of the way through your oration. You then deal rather better than you had expected with three or four questions and are surprised to hear that another fifteen minutes have gone by.

Back to the ante-room and the interminable wait while a succession of ballots is taken. At last after two or three false alarms the regional organizer of the party will come into the room, look at you straight in the eye and announce that Mr Y has been selected. You

[4] Nigel Nicolson, *People and Parliament* (London, Weidenfeld and Nicolson, 1958), p. 40.

shake hands with Mr Y and utter a few modest words of congratulation. Meanwhile that blithering idiot Mr Z is slapping Mr Y on the back and saying he had always known that Y would be chosen.

Back to the conference chamber with the other nominees. Deafening applause. The chairman says that all the nominees were absolutely first class (even if this was patently not the case). They would have liked to have chosen all of them, nevertheless they had to make a choice, however difficult, and the mantle had fallen on Mr Y. He was quite sure that such excellent people as Messrs W, X and Z would have no difficulty in being chosen soon by another constituency, and the members of his constituency would follow their future careers with interest. Then votes of thanks all round, a few words from the selected candidate and a final rousing call from the chairman to rally round and ensure that Mr Y becomes the next member for the constituency.

It is not easy for nominees to decide what to talk about in their set speeches. Should they talk about party policy or their personal records of work for the party? There is no set formula for success. The speech which would be an utter failure in constituency A may turn out an unqualified success in constituency B. All the nominee has to go on is his experience and the degree of his knowledge of local feeling. His main consolation is that all his rivals are confronted by the same dilemma.

Who is Chosen?

Looking at it from the other side, what are the members of the selection conference looking for in their candidate? This varies with the nature of the constituency, and especially according to the prospect of electoral success. If it is a marginal constituency the delegates are most likely to be impressed by the vote-winning prospects of their candidate and a pleasing personality would be the number one qualification. In a safe seat delegates are conscious of choosing the future Member rather than a candidate and are more concerned to choose a man with the requisite knowledge and experience to perform what they conceive to be the functions of an MP. In a hopeless constituency energy and enthusiasm count a great deal, and younger candidates are much more likely to be chosen.

Policy differences are relatively unimportant. It is commonly anticipated that left-wing constituency Labour parties are certain to select left-wing candidates and that right-wing Conservative associations, similarly, will pick extremist candidates. In fact, this happens much less frequently than is imagined. Selection conferences of all parties are more likely to pick the man or woman who "looks the part" rather than to insist on the nominee whose political views most exactly coincide with their own.

Local interests undoubtedly often play a part. If one is nominated for a farming constituency it is prudent to show some knowledge of and interest in agriculture, similarly with industrial areas where one industry is predominant. But in mixed industrial areas and especially in suburban constituencies there is likely to be more interest in national than in purely local issues.

Age may play an important part in deciding between nominees, though this again will vary very much. There are a few parties which would regard a man of fifty as a "young stripling," while others would regard a forty-year-old as a has-been. In general, the optimum age range is from thirty-five to forty-five, with a certain preference for younger candidates in hopeless and marginal seats and for older ones in safe constituencies.

Unlike in the United States and certain other countries, it is not customary for a candidate to be resident in the area which he seeks to represent. In fact the great majority of candidates in British Parliamentary elections are "carpet baggers" with no personal stake in the community they seek to represent. At some selection conferences it is a major advantage to be a local man, but equally often it can be a handicap. To come in from outside with no previous connections with local factions, can in many cases be a strong recommendation.

Regional prejudices seldom come into the picture in England, though in Scotland and Wales it is rare for a non-Scotsman or non-Welshman respectively to be chosen. Religion is not an important factor outside Northern Ireland, though Jews encounter strong prejudices in some local Conservative associations. In a few constituencies on Merseyside and in Glasgow Labour nominees who are Roman Catholics start with a distinct advantage.

A certain prejudice undoubtedly exists against women candidates, which is stronger in the Conservative Party than in the Labour Party and in rural areas than in towns. Many fewer women than men are selected and they tend to be chosen for the less hopeful seats.

In 1966 there were twenty-one Conservative women candidates out of 629, but of elected Conservative Members there were seven out of 253. At the same election Labour fielded thirty women candidates out of 621 and nineteen Labour women MPs were returned out of 363. There are undoubtedly many fewer women than men with Parliamentary ambitions but those who wish to be considered as candidates encounter stronger resistance than men. This, apparently, comes most often from their fellow women who are usually in a majority at Conservative selection conferences. A large number of these seem convinced that voters would be less likely to vote for a woman candidate than for a man.

The evidence for this belief is scanty. A Gallup poll taken in July 1952 revealed that 16 per cent of the voters thought that they would be less inclined to vote for a woman candidate, but this was partially offset by the 10 per cent who said they would be more inclined, 67 per cent saying that it would make no difference and 7 per cent expressing no opinion. On the basis of this poll it might be concluded that women candidates encountered a handicap of 6 per cent.

In practice it proves much less than this. The present author has made an exhaustive analysis of the results of the 1955 and 1959 elections, recording every constituency where a woman candidate in the 1955 election was replaced by a man of the same party in 1959 and vice versa, and comparing the results in these constituencies with the national trend.

The result of this analysis was that when a Conservative woman candidate had replaced a man, the pro-Conservative swing had averaged 0·4 per cent against a national average of 1·2 per cent. Where a Conservative man had replaced a woman candidate, the pro-Conservative swing was 1·6 per cent. This means that in the average constituency a woman Conservative candidate might expect to receive about 300 votes less than a man. The same analysis revealed no difference at all in the case of Labour candidates, while for Liberals and minor party candidates and independents the numbers involved were too small to point to any reliable conclusion. The analysis does suggest that there is a small minority of normally Conservative voters who will not vote for a woman candidate.[5]

It is not only women candidates who encounter difficulties in the Conservative Party. Despite frequent appeals from Central Office, culminating in a recommendation in the Selwyn Lloyd report of June 1963 that each selection conference should include one woman and one trade unionist among the nominees from which it makes its choice, it has proved virtually impossible to persuade Conserva-

[5] A similar analysis covering the 1964 and 1966 elections again showed that Conservative women candidates did worse than men. It also suggested that, in these later elections, Labour women candidates did slightly better than men. See *Daily Telegraph—Gallup Analysis of the Election '66* (London, *Daily Telegraph*, 1966), p. 27.

tive constituency associations to select working-class candidates. Only two Conservative MPs in the 1966 Parliament were working trade unionists when selected. Immediately after the 1966 election the then chairman of the Conservative Party, Edward du Cann, announced a tightening up of selection procedures in order to achieve a better and more representative choice of candidates. It remains to be seen whether this new initiative will prove more successful than others taken in the past.

The occupational backgrounds of candidates and elected members in the 1966 election are shown in Table 13:

Table 13—Occupational Backgrounds of Candidates, 1966

	Conservative		*Labour*		*Liberal*	
	Elected	*Defeated*	*Elected*	*Defeated*	*Elected*	*Defeated*
	%	%	%	%	%	%
Professions	47	48	43	50	50	48
Business	29	38	9	17	25	30
Miscellaneous	23	12	18	24	25	20
Workers	1	2	30	9	0	2

In the professions category the law, particularly the bar, is dominant in the Conservative and Liberal parties, and is very well represented in the Labour Party. There are a number of reasons for this. Traditionally the bar and politics have been associated professions. By virtue of their training and professional practice barristers are skilled at arguing a case and it may be expected that they would face a selection conference with more confidence than most. Barristers and solicitors, also, undoubtedly find it easier than most to organize their time in such a way that they can combine their profession with their Parliamentary work.

There is a fair sprinkling from the other professions among the candidates of all parties, but it is only teaching—at both school and university level—which comes near to challenging the predominance of the law. In fact, teachers form by far the largest occupational group among Labour candidates, nearly a quarter of whom in the 1966 general election were teachers, either at university, adult education or school level. In the Liberal Party, too, large numbers of candidates come from the teaching profession. Only a handful of Conservative candidates, however, are teachers—and those normally in unpromising constituencies.

It will come as a surprise to nobody to discover that business is largely represented in the Conservative Party and makes a good showing in the Liberal Party. The smaller number of Labour candidates with a business background are not really comparable, as a majority of these are small businessmen or employees of larger companies, often in junior positions, whereas a majority of the Conservatives in this category are company directors.

The largest groups in the miscellaneous category are farmers on the Conservative side and journalists in the Labour Party. Journalists, and especially public relations and advertising men are well represented in the Conservative and Liberal parties too. Amongst the workers, the largest group are the miners, who have practically a monopoly of Labour representation in coal-mining areas. Out of thirty-five miners who stood for Labour in 1966, no less than thirty-two were successful. A good proportion of the "workers" who stood in 1966 were full-time trade union officials, but the majority were working at their trades when first elected, and each general election brings to the Labour benches of the House of Commons reinforcements of members straight from the workbench. Most of these are sponsored candidates.

Only a derisory number of workers have at any time been selected as Conservative or Liberal candidates, and fewer still have been elected. In the Labour Party a majority of candidates would have been classified as workers in the period up to 1945 and a third of Labour MPs still fall in this category. But since that date the proportion of professional men (especially teachers) has greatly increased, and this has been largely at the expense of "workers." In very many cases the new aspirants have come from working-class families; but unlike their parents have enjoyed the benefits of a grammar school and/or university education. Ironically, workers stand a much better chance of being chosen to fight safe Labour seats rather than hopeless or marginal ones. This is because of the

Table 14—Background of MPs 1951 and 1966

	Conservative MPs		*Labour MPs*	
	1951	1966	1951	1966
	%	%	%	%
Occupation				
Professions	41	46	35	43
Business	37	29	9	9
Miscellaneous	22	23	19	18
Workers	—	—	37	30
Education				
Elementary	1	1	26	22
Secondary	24	18	50	60
Public School	75	80	20	18
(Eton)	(24)	(21)	(1)	(1)
Oxford and Cambridge	52	56	19	23
Other Universities	10	10	22	28

system of trade union sponsorship described on page 71 above. In 1966, 30 per cent of successful Labour candidates were workers, but only 9 per cent of unsuccessful ones. A more comprehensive analysis of the occupational background of candidates in 1966 is contained in the table in Appendix 7.

Table 14, reprinted from *The British General Election of 1966*, reveals how the composition of the House of Commons has altered over a fifteen-year period. The authors, David Butler and Anthony King, comment: "It seems that the Conservatives have gone on choosing the same sort of people, in social and economic terms at least. The Labour Party has changed its emphasis more; the result is an intellectually livelier Parliament but not necessarily a more representative one."[6]

In all parties there is a recognized route which the majority of would-be MPs are expected to follow. They must first fight a hopeless seat and, fortified by this salutary experience, they may then proceed to a marginal constituency and later, perhaps, to a safe one. A fair number of aspirants in both major parties, however, succeed in by-passing this route and secure election to the House of Commons at their first attempt.

How much influence have the party headquarters on the choice of candidates? It is clear that no HQ can force an individual on an unwilling constituency party. The most they can do is to try to persuade the constituency, through the regional organizer or agent, to include someone whom Transport House or the Central Office would like accommodated on the short list. Very often a constituency party is quite willing to accede to this, but it frequently happens that the constituency party executive committee will have other ideas about whom to include on the short list, and it is their view which prevails. Even when someone recommended from headquarters is included it is by no means always an advantage for this fact to be known. Once an officially recommended nominee is on the short list he takes his chance with everyone else.

The negative powers which the party headquarters possess to refuse endorsement to selected candidates are sparingly used. In the Labour Party, except in the rare case of someone who is clearly unsuited for personal reasons (such as the nominee for a Midlands constituency some years ago who, it later transpired, had recently been cashiered from the RAF for embezzling mess funds) it is in practice only used to exclude those with strong Communist or Trotskyist connections. In the Conservative and Liberal parties it

[6] *Op. cit.*, page 211.

is even rarer for selected candidates to be black-balled for political heterodoxy.[7]

How much security do prospective candidates enjoy? Not very much. Their relationship to their constituency parties is a delicate one. Disenchantment easily sets in on either side. This is not perhaps surprising, as candidate and constituency party have usually had only the most fleeting view of each other prior to selection.

Opportunities for disagreement abound. Parties and candidates often differ on how much work the candidate is expected to put in. It frequently happens that a prospective candidate visits the constituency less often than his party would like; less commonly parties may decide that they see altogether too much of their candidate. Changes in the personal position of the candidate may also occur. He may be offered a better job, or his employers may prove unexpectedly difficult about allowing time off. His health may suffer, or that of his family. He may take on other commitments which leave him less time for his candidature. Or he may wish to be considered for another, more promising constituency; so, for one reason or another, a sizeable number of prospective candidates withdraw "for personal reasons" long before polling day, and the procedure for selecting a new candidate has to be gone through all over again.

On the other hand, once a candidate has been elected as a Member he normally has no difficulty in retaining the support of his own party, and unless his seat is a marginal one, he normally continues to represent it, if he wishes, until the end of his working life. It is extremely difficult for a constituency party to rid itself of an unwanted Member, the required procedure for doing this in both the Conservative and Labour parties being weighted heavily on the side of the Member. Surprisingly, in view of the fact that political differences are usually stronger in the Labour Party, it is constituency Conservative associations who more frequently attempt to unseat a Member with whom they disagree. Such efforts, however, are normally unsuccessful and it is rare for more than one or two Members to be forced out by their constituencies during the course of a Parliament.

[7] An exhaustive account of the procedures for selecting Parliamentary candidates is given in Austin Ranney, *Pathways to Parliament* (Madison, University of Wisconsin Press; and London, Macmillan, 1965.) His view is that "the national organizations' actual influence over candidate selection is substantially weaker than their formal supervisory powers allow." He concludes: "while British national party organizations play distinctly more active roles than their American counterparts in the selection of candidates for national offices, the great majority of the choices have been made in 'law' and in fact by the constituency organizations."

An exception was the aftermath of the Suez operation, when feelings were running extremely high and four Conservatives and one Labour Member lost the support of their constituency parties. Two of these resigned their seats forthwith, the others were replaced by more orthodox party candidates at the subsequent general election.[8]

Many members of constituency parties would like their Members to behave as delegates of the party rather than as representatives of the constituency, but they have little opportunity to enforce their will. Each of the three major parties sets its face firmly against such a conception of a Member's responsibilities, the Labour and Liberal parties implicitly, the Conservative Party explicitly. The Central Office pamphlet *Notes on Procedure for the Adoption of Conservative Candidates in England and Wales* quotes Burke, with approval: "Your representative owes you not his industry only, but his judgment; and he betrays instead of serving you if he sacrifices it to your opinion... authoritative instructions, which the Member is bound blindly and implicitly to obey, though contrary to the dearest convictions of his judgment and conscience, are utterly unknown to the laws of the land, and against the tenor of our constitution."

In practice, few Members encounter serious difficulties with their constituency parties over policy matters, though disagreements are frequent. It is rare for a Member who deviates towards an extreme position on the outside edge, as it were, of his party, to run into trouble with his constituency party. This is because constituency parties are normally more extreme than the party leadership. Members who deviate towards the centre may, however, find themselves in difficulty. It is not surprising that none of the Suez rebels on the right of the Conservative Party found themselves out of step with their constituency association, though four out of the five Conservative Members who most strongly opposed the original attack on Egypt were disowned by their associations. Conversely, in the Labour Party right-wing deviants are much more likely than left-wingers to meet trouble in their constituency parties. In general, however, the vast majority of constituency parties accept, however reluctantly, that they are unable to dictate the political line of their Members. It is in most cases a more serious matter for a Member to be out of step with his party leadership in the House of Commons than to be in disagreement with the members of his constituency party.

[8] See also L. D. Epstein, "British M.P.s and their Local Parties: The Suez Case," *American Political Science Review*, Vol. LIV, No. 2, June, 1960.

8. The Campaign in the Constituencies

THE ANNOUNCEMENT BY THE PRIME MINISTER OF AN IMPENDING general election precipitates a flurry of activity in constituency and local party branches throughout the country. Emergency meetings are hastily convened to put the local party machines on a "wartime footing" and to make arrangements for the formal adoption of Parliamentary candidates.

If, as happened in 1955, the dissolution is announced unexpectedly a fair number of constituency parties may find themselves without a prospective candidate, but even when the election is anticipated a handful of parties find themselves in the same position because of the recent resignation of their previously selected candidates. A few other prospective candidates are likely to find, when the dissolution is announced, that an election campaign at that particular time would be inconvenient and they therefore withdraw from the field. All in all, it is unlikely that fewer than half a dozen candidates have to be found at short notice at any general election by each of the Labour and Conservative parties, and in such circumstances the selection procedures outlined in Chapter 7 are telescoped considerably.

The Liberal Party and each of the minor parties usually have to find a higher proportion of their candidates at this stage. In many constituencies a decision to fight has been left in abeyance and the first question to be resolved at their emergency meetings is whether a candidate is to be put into the field at all. (The Conservative and Labour parties normally fight virtually every seat as a matter of principle, though on occasions both parties have allowed the Speaker a free run. The only other exceptions in recent times for the Labour Party are a few county constituencies in Northern Ireland where Labour is exceptionally weak. Conservative candidates have occasionally stood down in a few constituencies to enable Liberals to have a straight fight with Labour, though this has not happened since 1959.)

In deciding whether to put up a candidate, a constituency party will seriously consider not only its potential voting strength in the area and the availability of a suitable man or woman to stand, but its financial position. A deposit of £150 is required to be paid to the Returning Officer at the time of nomination, and this is returnable only if the candidate polls more than one-eighth of the total vote. In addition, a minimum of £250, and preferably at least £500, is needed if an adequate campaign is to be mounted.

As soon as the question of a candidate is resolved the election agent, who is the key figure in every campaign, is appointed. The position is a statutory one and every candidate is required to notify the name and address of the person appointed, in writing, to the returning officer. The election agent is legally responsible for authorizing all expenditure on behalf of a candidature and his name must appear as the publisher on all printed material, including posters and window bills, issued in support of the candidate. His official duties do not end until he has sent in a return of election expenses to the returning officer after the result of the election has been declared.

A candidate may act as his own election agent, though this rarely happens except in the case of independents and minor party candidates. When a constituency party employs a full-time agent, he automatically takes on the job. Otherwise it is assumed by an experienced member of the local party. Most "amateur" agents arrange to take at least three weeks off from their regular work to devote themselves to their electoral duties. The work of an election agent is extremely arduous, beginning early in the morning and continuing far into the night, at least during the three weeks prior to polling day. His wife and family can expect to see almost nothing of him during this time.

Once the question of a candidate and an agent have been settled, there is little more for a governing body of a constituency party to do. It is usual for a "campaign committee," consisting of a handful of key workers prepared to devote virtually all their spare time to the election, to be appointed to supervise the details of the campaign, in conjunction with the agent and candidate. A financial appeal will be issued to members and known sympathizers and the agent will be authorized to spend up to a specified sum during the campaign. The party will then pass a resolution either formally dissolving itself or suspending all public propaganda activities for the duration of the election. The purpose of this is to emphasize that all activities on behalf of the candidature during the election period are the personal responsibility of the agent.

The first task of the agent is to obtain premises suitable for use as a campaign headquarters or central committee rooms, as they are called. When the party itself owns permanent premises which are suitable for this purpose there is no problem. Otherwise a frantic search is mounted for vacant shop or office premises, preferably in a prominent position in the main street of the principal town in the constituency. Labour candidates often experience great difficulties in obtaining premises of this kind because of the hostility of private commercial interests, but this is partly offset by the willingness of co-operative societies to make accommodation available. A high proportion of Labour committee rooms are housed above co-operative stores.

If commercial premises cannot be found or the party cannot afford to pay for them the committee rooms are likely to be established in the front room of a private house of a keen party member. The keenness of such a member will certainly be put to a severe test in such circumstances, for neither he nor his family is likely to be afforded much privacy in the succeeding weeks. Sub-committee rooms in each ward or polling district will also be set up; these will nearly always be in private houses.

Once established in his committee rooms, the agent is confronted with a bewildering multiplicity of duties. These come easily to the old hand, but to the inexperienced they can pose formidable problems. Fortunately, the party headquarters run excellent correspondence courses for those likely to be appointed as temporary agents and also publish handbooks setting out clearly the legal responsibilities of election agents and giving detailed guidance as to how their duties should be carried out. In case of difficulty a call to the party's regional organizer should elicit sound advice. The agent of an independent or minor party candidate is denied such help, and in practice it is he who is most likely to come unstuck. A prudent man in such a position would swallow his pride and equip himself with one of the agent's handbooks published by the major parties and freely on sale from their headquarters.

An election agent is unlikely to find himself short of willing helpers. The hard core of active party workers will devote the greater part of their spare time during evenings and weekends to the campaign, and they are likely to be supplemented by a larger number of normally inactive members who feel that they ought to rally round at election time. Many sympathetic members of the public, too, who are unwilling to become party members, will turn up at the committee rooms and offer to lend a hand. To keep this motley array of helpers happy and purposefully occupied requires high qualities of tact and diplomacy.

All the varied tasks undertaken by the election agent and his team of helpers are directed towards three objects: to familiarize the name of the candidate and underline his party affiliation, to identify the party's supporters within the constituency and to build up a machine capable of ensuring the maximum turn-out of these supporters on election day.

The first object would be less necessary if the existence of political parties was recognized more extensively in election law. In fact, no mention of a candidate's party affiliation is made on the ballot paper, so it is up to the parties to familiarize the electors with the names of their candidates. Hence, all election literature and posters and window bills give great prominence to linking the candidate's name with his party. JONES FOR LABOUR or VOTE SMITH, CONSERVATIVE X are slogans which become increasingly familiar to every voter, as polling day approaches.

The activities of the candidate during the election campaign are a continuation and intensification of the work which he has been doing in the constituency in the months and years leading up to the election. The main difference is that the word "prospective" is at last dropped from his title and that the public can now be asked to "Vote for Jones" instead of merely for the party. The transition is usually marked by an adoption meeting, held as soon as possible after the election is announced, at which the candidature is formally proclaimed. This is usually a public meeting, which every party member is strongly urged to attend, as a demonstration of enthusiasm and confidence. Speeches are made by the candidate and several other speakers, an appeal for financial support is made and a resolution formally adopting the candidate may be formally put to the meeting. It need hardly be added that such a resolution is invariably carried with acclamation. If the candidate is the retiring Member of Parliament for the constituency he will by this time have dropped the MP from his name, as he has ceased to be a Member since the dissolution of Parliament. During the election campaign he is merely a candidate and his status is no different from that of the other candidates in the constituency.

The adoption has no legal standing and each candidate must be formally nominated in writing. Nominations may be made on any day after the publication by the returning officer of the date of the election but not later than the eighth day after the date of the Proclamation summoning the new Parliament. This gives, in practice, a period of five days in which nominations may be made, and the final day for nominations is also the final day on which a nomination may be withdrawn.

The nomination form must be signed by a proposer and seconder and by eight other people, all of whom must be electors for the constituency in which the candidate is to stand. The nomination form contains the candidate's full name, address and "description" (or profession) and his proposers must sign their names in the same form in which they are listed in the election register and must also add their electoral numbers.

Only one nomination form is required but it is usual for an agent to arrange for several to be filled in by different electors, partly as an insurance against one form being invalid and partly as a demonstration of support for his candidate.

The nomination form or forms must be delivered in person to the returning officer by the candidate or his proposer or seconder between the hours of 10 a.m. and 3 p.m. on one of the days when nominations may be made. The nomination must be accompanied by the £150 deposit, and by the candidate's consent in writing to nomination, which must be attested by one witness.

Provided a nomination paper has been filled in and delivered exactly as described above it will be deemed valid by the returning officer. Representatives of candidates may inspect the nomination papers of their rivals and may lodge objections if they suspect them to be invalid. The returning officer must then give his decision as soon as possible and if he decides that a nomination paper is invalid he must endorse the paper as invalid and state on it the reasons for his decision. This does not happen at all frequently, and when it does there is normally time for the candidate to send in another nomination paper which is correctly filled in, as few candidates are so imprudent as to leave their nomination to the very last moment.

If by the time that nominations are closed only one valid nomination has been received, the returning officer declares that person elected and publishes notices to that effect throughout the constituency.[1] Where there are at least two candidates, as happens in the vast majority of cases, the returning officer publishes a statement of persons nominated, together with the names of their proposers, seconders and assentors. This statement includes a notice of the poll, stating the date and time that the election is to be held, and gives particulars as to where people should go to vote. By this time things are hotting up; it is a mere nine days (excluding Sundays and Bank holidays) to polling day.

At least a fortnight before polling day, and probably a week or two earlier, the candidate will have moved into the constituency for the duration of the campaign. Unless he normally lives there,

[1] The most recent unopposed returns were in 1951.

he will take a room at a hotel or lodge with one of his supporters. If he is married his wife will accompany him, family circumstances permitting, and she will be expected to take an active part in his campaign. Some idea of their daily life during the three weeks before polling day is given by the following imaginary timetable of a candidate in a county constituency.

7.30 a.m. Get up. Breakfast. Read all the papers—especially reports of the speeches of the party leaders and other election news.

8.30–9.30. Work in hotel bedroom on speeches to be delivered in the evening.

9.30. Meet reporter from local newspaper at hotel. Comment on speech given by rival candidate on previous day.

9.50. Arrive main committee rooms, in car driven by wife. Dictate replies to correspondence received from electors. Quick consultation with the agent on the day's programme.

10.30. Set off with woman councillor for door-to-door canvass of housewives on new housing estate.

12 noon. Visit hospital with wife to meet patients. Talk with matron to check that arrangements for postal votes for the patients have been made.

1 p.m. Quick lunch in café.

1.30. Drive to town at other end of constituency.

2.15. Set off on loudspeaker tour—making short speeches and answering questions at street corners.

3.15. Wife leaves to have tea with the Townswomen's Guild.

4.30. Meet a deputation of Roman Catholics to hear their case for more public money to maintain Catholic schools.

5.30. Speak to factory gate meeting.

6.30. Return to main committee rooms, immediately set off with agent for quick tour of sub-committee rooms.

7.30. Supper at home of party chairman.

8.15. Leave for first of three village meetings.

9.45. Return to town hall for main evening meeting, which has already been addressed by a prominent visiting speaker.

10.15. Adjourn to pub with party supporters.

11.30. Return to hotel and to bed.

This kind of pace is sustained without much difficulty by nearly all candidates,[2] though elderly men who are defending safe seats

[2] In an earlier edition of this book the author described the above programme as "a cracking pace." This provoked an astonished reaction from a leading political scientist who wrote: "American visitors are always amazed by the soft lives that British politicians lead. This, by American standards, would be an easy day." On the other hand, the author was lightheartedly

tend to take it a lot easier. The constant excitement and the enthusiastic encouragement of supporters go a long way to create fresh reserves of energy which the candidate would not previously have suspected himself of possessing. A major problem is to restrain the ardour of one's supporters who will quite happily keep one up talking all night. Here a firm intervention by the candidate's wife is indicated.

It is notable how little the campaigns of rival candidates impinge on each other. The candidates may meet once or twice on neutral ground—at a meeting for all candidates organized by the United Nations Association, perhaps, or at an inter-denominational service held for election workers. One candidate may take up some remarks of another, as reported in the local newspaper, and reply to them at one of his meetings or challenge the accuracy of his facts. Very occasionally a candidate may make a personal attack on his rival, but this is normally regarded as bad form and is likely to do the attacker more harm than good.

The great majority of candidates, however, totally ignore the existence of their rivals throughout the campaign. If they are government supporters they will doggedly defend the record of the government with an occasional side swipe at the irresponsibility of the opposition, but if any names are mentioned, it will be of well-known national leaders rather than the opposition's local standard bearer. The same is broadly true, in reverse, of opposition candidates, though a former Member defending his seat is more likely to be picked out by name than a newly arrived challenger.[3]

Although they are rarely attended by more than 200–300 people, except when a party leader is one of the speakers, and in fact the *average* audience is probably not more than 10 per cent of this size, public meetings normally constitute by far the most interesting and colourful events in the candidate's timetable.

There are certain superficial differences between meetings held by the opposing parties. At Conservative meetings the platform is invariably draped with Union Jacks, for which the Labour Party

rebuked by a well-known Labour M.P., now a member of the Wilson Cabinet. "Before your book appeared," he said, "I had always succeeded in persuading my agent that candidates could not be expected to do any electioneering before lunchtime. Now he has me out canvassing after breakfast!"

[3] For an account of how candidates, themselves, view election campaigning, based on answers to a questionnaire sent to candidates in the 1966 election, see Richard Rose and Denis Kavanagh, "Campaigning for Parliament," in *New Society*, 28 July, 1966.

substitutes banners proclaiming party slogans. Tory meetings often conclude with the singing of "God Save the Queen," a display of patriotism which is considered inappropriate by the other parties. A collection is invariably taken at Labour and Liberal meetings, less frequently at Conservative ones.

In other respects the pattern is fairly uniform. The speeches vary greatly in style and content, but more through differences in the background and experience of the speakers than because of political differences. The younger and less experienced they are, the more likely are they to keep pretty close to their brief—which in most cases is based on speaker's notes distributed by the various party headquarters. Local issues are likely to be stressed by town councillors and others—particularly when the opposing candidate is a stranger in the district.

The arrival of the candidate is heralded by a round of applause from his own supporters and perhaps some good-humoured banter from the other side. If the opposition is well represented in the audience a more lively and interesting meeting is likely to ensue. Hostile questions test the mettle of a candidate far more than the polite enquiries he receives from his own supporters, and at many meetings "enemy intervention" extends to the interruption or "heckling" of the speaker. A speaker who is quick and nimble-witted enough to score debating points against hecklers, without losing the thread of his speech, adds greatly to his stature. It is not common for heckling to get seriously out of hand but it occasionally does happen, especially in marginal constituencies where feeling is running high. In such cases it may be almost impossible for the speakers to make themselves heard and the chairman is forced to appeal for order. If he is wise he will do this in a good-humoured manner, appealing to the opponents' sportsmanship and belief in free speech and emphasizing that questions will be welcomed at a later stage in the evening.

If such an appeal is ignored the chairman is placed in a tricky position. He can ask his stewards to eject people making a disturbance, but if the "enemy" contingent is large this could prove a difficult job. He can swallow his pride and ignore the continued disorder in the hope that the speaker will eventually succeed in getting his message across. Or he can solemnly remind the audience that any person acting in a disorderly manner at a public meeting for the purpose of preventing the transaction of business is liable to a fine or imprisonment and announce that he is sending for a police constable to ensure that the law is enforced. This final course of action is virtually certain to succeed in its purpose, at any rate when the constable has arrived, but it is normally regarded as a moral defeat for the platform and is rarely resorted to.

While the candidate is straining every effort to make himself known to as many voters as possible, the agent is equally busy ensuring that contact is established with every potential supporter of the party in the constituency. If the party organization is good he will have started the campaign with a marked-up register covering the greater part of the constituency. In that case he will ask his team of canvassers to call on all the "F" (for) voters to confirm that they are party supporters and on the "D" or doubtful voters to see if they have moved off the fence. Those voters marked "A" (against) are left firmly alone. Many agents find that no reasonably up-to-date canvassing records are in existence and they have to instruct their canvassers to call on every voter. In either case canvassing is regarded as much the most important single activity which has to be undertaken during elections, and every available person is pressed into service. It is normal for canvassing teams to go out on every evening of the campaign and in the daytime during weekends. Theoretically, parties aim to make a 100 per cent canvas of the constituency, but most agents are more than pleased if their canvassers call on 80 per cent of the voters. It is normal to begin with the most favourable parts of the constituency and move on later to the less promising areas: so if, as often happens, a party canvasses only 50 per cent of the voters it may have called on 75 per cent of its own supporters.

In a marginal constituency it is prudent to set a target of 2,000 or 3,000 more favourable promises than would be necessary to win the seat. Most canvassers, particularly inexperienced ones who are much in evidence at election time, are incurably optimistic and are liable to read into a courteous reception a promise of support. It is this rather than deliberate deception which most often leads to voters being recorded in the "F" column by canvassers representing opposing candidates. Whatever the reason, it is certain that nine candidates out of ten receive an inflated estimate of support from their canvassers.

Canvassers are asked to undertake a number of subsidiary jobs. They are liberally supplied with window bills to offer to supporters, and they are instructed to enquire about elderly or infirm voters who might require a lift to the poll or, if there is still time, to be assisted in applying for a postal vote. Canvassers are also often given leaflets to deliver "on their rounds." It is important for canvassers to ask to see every voter on the register at each house at which they call, and not to assume that the person who comes to the door speaks for the whole household. More families than most people imagine are divided in their voting habits, and households containing lodgers are unlikely to be politically homogeneous. A high proportion of canvassers, however, despite the instructions of their agents, take the easy way out and do not bother to interview all members of a household. This is a further source of gross inaccuracies in canvassing records.

After canvassing the next biggest campaign chore is the addressing of envelopes for the candidate's election address. In most constituencies some 50,000–60,000 are required and this places a severe strain on the weaker constituency organizations. It is usual to ask each ward or local branch to be responsible for addressing the envelopes for its own area and each active member is given a quota of anything from fifty to one thousand envelopes to address, together with the appropriate portion of the election register. Elderly and housebound people who are not available for canvassing and other outdoor work are often happy to volunteer to receive a large batch of envelopes. If the election occurs in the fifth year of the Parliament some parties will already have got their envelopes addressed before the campaign begins, as they could be sure the election would be fought on the current register. Only a minority normally shows such foresight.

The election address is the traditional means by which the candidate introduces himself to the electorate. It normally contains a photograph of the candidate, and perhaps also of his wife and children, biographical details, a personal message in which he promises to devote himself to the service of the electors should he be elected and a summary of his party's programme. Often it will include a short message from the candidate's wife, addressed to women voters.

The post office is obliged at Parliamentary elections to make one free delivery to every elector on behalf of each candidate, and the great majority of candidates take advantage of this to send out their election addresses.

Serious doubt is often cast on whether the trouble and expenditure devoted by candidates to their election addresses is really worth while. Most candidates in fact spend between a quarter and half of their permitted expenditure on their election address. According to the opinion polls, however, more electors are reached by means of the election address than by any other *local* form of electioneering. In 1966 the Gallup poll reported that 49 per cent of electors had looked at election addresses, while the National Opinion Poll (NOP) found that 31 per cent had been canvassed and only 4 per cent claimed to have attended political meetings.

An agent who has the assistance of an able and experienced election committee to which he is willing to delegate a great deal of responsibility, should find that, though he will work hard and for very long hours, his campaign will run fairly smoothly. One who is unable or unwilling to delegate is likely to find himself prey to constant crises. Ideally, each member of the election committee should be allocated responsibility for one specific field of duties, allowing the agent to free himself for the general oversight of the campaign. There should be a canvassing officer, another in charge of speakers, one responsible for the addressing of envelopes, one for dealing with the Press, one in charge of leaflet distribution, one for organizing cars for election day and one to organize the postal vote. The agent will probably reserve for himself the planning of the candidate's timetable and it is important that a fixed time be set aside each day for consultation between the candidate and the agent.

Planning the schedule of meetings is especially complicated in county constituencies where the candidate may easily be addressing six village meetings every evening, rounding them off with a larger meeting in one of the towns. Each meeting requires at least one or two supporting speakers, whose main qualification must be the ability to modify drastically the length of their speeches. It inevitably happens that on some evenings the candidate gets seriously held up at his earlier meetings and arrives at his final meeting anything up to an hour and a half late. A supporting speaker booked to speak for twenty minutes has consequently to spin out his speech or fill in the time answering questions. On another day, he will find that the candidate arrives at the meeting just as he has completed his introductory remarks and is about to embark on the main body of his speech. In that case he must cut himself short and make way for the candidate, with as little delay as possible.

Most agents are well conversant with electoral law and are aware of the things which may or may not be done during an election campaign. A much less detailed store of knowledge is normally possessed by voluntary workers, and care must be taken that through ignorance or misguided enthusiasm they do not transgress the law. If they do, they may lay themselves open, and possibly also the agent and the candidate, to heavy penalties and even to the invalidation of the election should their candidate be elected. A summary of election offences, with the penalties involved should be prominently displayed in all committee rooms.

In practice people involved in electioneering in Britain have proved extremely law abiding and after each general election there are never more than a handful of prosecutions for election offences.

The last time an election was invalidated because of an election offence was at Oxford in 1924. In Northern Ireland respect for the election laws is perhaps rather less strongly ingrained and attempts at personation (voting in the name of some other person) are not infrequent. Each party in Northern Ireland appoints special "personation agents" who keep a close watch at each polling station to deter supporters of the other side from "stealing" votes in this way. But even in Northern Ireland stories of attempted personation are probably greatly exaggerated.[4] A summary of election offences and of the penalties involved is included in Appendix 6.

Especially in marginal constituencies, agents make daily reports by telephone to their regional organizers, who are also likely to make at least one personal visit. The regional officers of both the Labour and Conservative parties do their best to organize the transfer of workers from safe and hopeless into marginal constituencies so that the maximum effort can be mounted where it will have the greatest effect. As a much higher proportion of their active members are car owners and therefore more mobile, it is clear that the Conservatives have less trouble in organizing such transfers and they are in fact able to effect them on a much larger scale.

As polling day draws near the tempo of the campaign appreciably quickens. More helpers turn up every day at the committee rooms and enthusiasm and confidence mounts. Almost all voluntary election workers and most professional ones become infected with over-optimism towards the end of the campaign, unless their own party is very obviously doing badly. It is normal to over-estimate the chances both of one's candidate in the constituency and of one's party throughout the country. It would indeed be strange if it were otherwise, for so much is seen of the results of one's own campaigning and so little of the other side's that it is all but impossible to form an objective view.

A week before polling day most agents make a rapid assessment of the progress already made in canvassing and other important activities and revise their plans accordingly.

Targets may be raised or lowered, or forces concentrated to recall at houses where the voters were "out" or "doubtful" on the first occasion that they were canvassed. All election workers are likely to be impressed at this stage by how much remains to be done and how little time is left in which to do it.

[4] See Desmond G. Neill, "The Election in Northern Ireland," in D. E. Butler, *The British General Election of 1951* (London, Macmillan, 1952), pp. 220–35, and Cornelius O'Leary, "Belfast West," in Butler and King (1966), *op. cit.*, pp. 254–58.

Meanwhile, the agent's attention will be more and more concentrated on preparations for polling day. The transporting of elderly and disabled voters to the polls (and of many others who are unlikely themselves to summon up enough energy to get themselves there unaided) can add several hundred votes to a candidate's poll. Every effort is therefore made to secure the services of the maximum number of cars and drivers on election day and, especially, in the evening. It is illegal to hire transport for this purpose and party members who are owner drivers are strongly encouraged to volunteer their services.

Between 1948 and 1958 there was a legal restriction on the number of cars which a candidate could use for this purpose and each car had to be registered with the returning officer in advance. The number of cars allowed was one per candidate for every 2,500 electors in boroughs and one for every 1,500 in counties. The purpose of the restriction was to prevent a party which had a preponderance of wealthy supporters from turning this fact to its advantage. It was repealed by a Conservative government in 1958, on the grounds that the increasing incidence of car ownership at once reduced the party advantage involved and made the law difficult to enforce. Although the Conservatives have undoubtedly benefited from the repeal of this restriction, the arguments which they advanced carry considerable weight and it is unlikely that a future Labour government would seek to reintroduce control in this field.

As well as compiling a roster of cars and drivers for election day, the agent will endeavour to persuade as many helpers as possible to take the day off work, so that a full-scale operation can be mounted to "get out the vote." Particularly in marginal constituencies, little difficulty is encountered in ensuring an adequate army of helpers on the big day.

Meanwhile, the returning officer will be busy with his own preparations. Soon after the nominations are closed he will send out, through the post office, to each elector, an official poll card. This will notify the voter of his electoral number and tell him how, where and when to vote. In the presence of the candidates, or more likely their representatives, he will also send out ballot papers to registered postal voters. In the average constituency there are about one thousand of these (or roughly 2 per cent of the electorate), though the number varies widely. Each postal voter is sent, by post, four items, *viz.*:

(1) An ordinary ballot paper, duly marked or stamped.
(2) A form of declaration of identity.

(3) A small envelope for the ballot paper.
(4) A larger addressed return envelope.

The postal voter must sign the declaration of identity, and have his signature attested by one witness. He marks his X against the candidate of his choice, seals his ballot paper in the small envelope and returns it, together with the declaration of identity, in the larger envelope. The vote can be sent back to the returning officer at any time after it has been recorded, but it must reach him not later than 9 p.m. on polling day. On their receipt at the office of the returning officer the postal votes are dropped into a special ballot box.

The returning officer, like the agents, has to make arrangements to secure the services of a large number of assistants on polling day. Some of them will be polling clerks, whose duty will consist of presiding over polling stations. Others will have the job of counting the votes. Unlike the parties' election workers, the returning officer's staff will be paid for their services. The greater number of them will be local government employees, transferred for the day from other work. They will be supplemented by others engaged specially for the day. School-teachers are a favourite source of labour for polling clerks, as most schools have a holiday on election day because their premises are used as polling stations. Bank clerks, for obvious reasons, are much in demand to assist in counting the votes.

9. The National Campaign

FIFTY YEARS AGO ELECTION CAMPAIGNS WERE CONDUCTED ALMOST exclusively at a constituency level. Apart from organizing speaking tours by the party leaders and other prominent personalities, the party headquarters played little direct part in the campaign. The newspapers were full of election news, but they were read only by a minority, and a far greater readership was claimed by regional and local papers than is the case today.

The irruption of mass readership national newspapers and, even more, the development of radio and television has changed all that. A general election was formerly a series of local contests to choose Members of Parliament, with the incidental effect of determining the political complexion of the next government. Now it is, in effect, a nationwide contest to choose a government and especially a prime minister. The fact that 630 individuals are in the same process elected to represent 630 different constituencies in Parliament has become a subordinate feature. This is the main reason why, as is shown in Chapter 13, there is so little variation in the results obtained in different constituencies—even in the case of those separated by hundreds of miles.

Unlike the majority of constituency parties, which are overwhelmingly dependent on voluntary labour, the party headquarters, staffed by full-time professionals, are not likely to be caught seriously unprepared by the announcement of a general election, even if it has come unexpectedly. Much of the work on which their employees have been engaged for several years past has been designed with this very moment in mind.

Increasingly in recent elections the party machines have concentrated on pre-electoral propaganda which has been launched well in advance of the date of the election. These have largely taken the form of colourful posters displayed on hoardings throughout the country, but particularly in marginal seats, and of advertisements in a large number of national and daily newspapers (political advertising on television and radio being illegal). The Conservatives' pre-electoral campaign before the 1959 election, was launched two full years earlier, in the autumn of 1957, and cost over £450,000. Before the 1964 election both major parties began their propaganda campaigns seventeen months in advance—in May 1963—and on this occasion the Conservatives spent one million pounds and Labour over £300,000.[1] Private business interests, allied to the Conservatives, spent even larger sums on similar campaigns. In 1966, however, there were no pre-election campaigns because of the high degree of uncertainty about the timing of the election, which might theoretically have been postponed until as late as October 1969. The money expended in these campaigns is not subject to the official limitation on election expenditure, as they are terminated when the dissolution of Parliament is announced. Paradoxically, the beginning of a campaign is now invariably the cue for covering up or taking down political posters, which otherwise would be liable to be charged as election expenditure.

When the dissolution is announced the party headquarters are well prepared to produce within a few days speakers' handbooks, outlining the party policy on a wide range of issues and documenting the failures of the opposing parties, which are quickly despatched to all Parliamentary candidates and others who are to speak on behalf of the party. These handbooks are supplemented by daily briefings on specific issues which arise during the course of the campaign. A great mass of posters, leaflets, policy statements and other propaganda material is also produced for distribution through the constituency party organizations. Some of the money subscribed to the national election funds of the parties is also disbursed to constituency parties, at this stage, to ensure that even the poorest of these have some ready cash with which to finance their campaign. In recent elections the Liberals have not been able to extend such monetary help to their constituency branches. It is usual at the beginning of the campaign for the party leadership to depute two or three senior figures to remain in London to oversee the running of the party headquarters and to act as a campaign committee, co-ordinating the day-to-day running of the campaign and particularly to take charge of the party's television programmes and dealings with the Press. It is usual to select MPs representing safe seats for this important assignment, as those with marginal constituencies could hardly be expected to leave them for the greater part of the campaign. For the same reason, in the cases of the Conservatives

[1] See Chapter 14, below. Two recent books describe these campaigns in great detail. *Communication and Political Power* by Lord Windlesham (London, Cape, 1966) deals with the Conservative campaigns in 1959 and 1964. *Influencing Voters* by Richard Rose, *op. cit.,* describes all the campaigns leading up to the 1964 election.

and the Liberals, leading peers are often included in their campaign committees.

Within a few days of the announcement of the dissolution, each party publishes its election manifesto. This is a statement of the issues which the party considers of the greatest importance and an indication, in more or less precise terms, of the party's policies to meet them. The Labour Party, which is strongly wedded to the idea that a party winning an election receives a mandate from the people to carry out definite policies, is normally more specific in its proposals.

The manifestos, which run to about two to three thousand words, are given the widest possible distribution, the print orders running into millions. In addition to the large scale distribution through constituency parties, they form the basis of the policy sections in candidates' election addresses and they are widely reported in the Press and on radio and television.

Despite the prominence which they are accorded, the election manifestos are seldom notable for breaking new ground. Nearly all the major proposals contained in past manifestos had already been published as official party policy and the function of the manifestos was to bring them together in a sharp and challenging manner and perhaps to add a few minor twists to give them an air of originality. In 1966 none of the three manifestos—*Time for Decision* (Labour), *Action Not Words* (Conservative) and *For All The People* (Liberal) —contained any substantial new policy proposal.

The issues which are discussed during election campaigns obviously differ to some extent on each occasion, but certain subjects, such as the economy, housing, education and pensions, are likely to be raised by all parties at every election. Table 15, which analyzes the subjects mentioned in candidates' election addresses in the 1964 and 1966 elections, gives a good idea of the range of ideas discussed, and of the way in which the emphasis changed from 1964, when a Conservative government was seeking re-election, to 1966, when a Labour government was defending its record. The table also shows the relatively small emphasis placed on foreign policy and defence issues. This does not reflect the importance which candidates place on these issues (which are often in the forefront of their minds), but the low level of public interest which successive opinion polls have confirmed.

The election addresses are normally composed at least three weeks before election day and do not reflect the issues which arise spontaneously during the campaign. There were relatively few of these in 1966, which however was unusual in that the Conservative oppo-

Table 15—Issues in 1964 and 1966

Subjects mentioned in candidates' addresses (1964 percentages in brackets)	Cons. %	Lab. %	Lib. %
General			
Mention of own party leader	19 (41)	47 (8)	16 (31)
Attack on Con. misrule—1964	—	32 (24)	30 (26)
Attack on Lab. misrule—1964–66	56	—	33
Slogan: "Action not words"	47	—	—
"You know lab. government works"	—	69	—
Social Questions			
Education	66 (89)	71 (93)	60 (90)
Health—general policy	25 (55)	42 (58)	14 (30)
Abolition of prescription charges	—	40 (50)	—
Reintroduction of prescription charges	9	—	—
Pensions	70 (90)	86 (86)	56 (87)
Housing—general policy	74 (85)	87 (90)	60 (74)
Rents, Rent Act	29 (10)	79 (86)	33 (87)
Home ownership	40 (33)	74 (86)	46 (57)
Immigration	11 (8)	— (14)	— (3)
Crime	40	—	2
Reintroduce capital punishment	6	—	—
The Economy			
Prosperity, cost and standard of living	69 (89)	69 (65)	67 (51)
State of economy, exports, trade	53 (60)	73 (69)	67 (31)
Employment, unemployment	8 (63)	16 (30)	5 (10)
Taxation, rates	77 (60)	42 (41)	67 (64)
Nationalization	14 (63)	13 (27)	33 (30)
Trade unions, industrial relations	62 (24)	8 (5)	44 (24)
Monopolies, restrictive practices	27 (22)	6 (34)	39 (56)
Transport	29 (49)	21 (49)	26 (33)
Agriculture	20 (34)	11 (30)	26 (41)
Regional development	21 (26)	26 (39)	60 (50)
Co-ownership	—	—	52 (80)
World Affairs			
Nuclear weapons policy	6 (83)	2 (58)	7 (60)
Negotiation of test-ban treaty	5 (31)	14 (—)	19 (—)
Other defence	38 (14)	35 (50)	44 (62)
Europe	50 (11)	9 (8)	67 (38)
Aid to developing countries	2 (20)	10 (27)	1 (15)
United Nations	6 (8)	23 (43)	30 (55)
Commonwealth	5 (35)	2 (37)	— (31)
Rhodesia	44	15	21
East of Suez	11	1	31
No mention of foreign affairs	15 (7)	48 (22)	1 (52)

This table is based on an analysis of the addresses of Conservative, Labour and Liberal candidates from a random sample of one-fifth of the constituencies in England, Scotland and Wales. A simple mention of any of these topics, however brief, was recorded. It is not to suggest, of course, that party attitudes on these questions were the same. (This table was first published in Butler and King (1966), *op. cit.*, p. 103.)

sition's record was discussed almost as widely as that of the Labour Government. This was because Labour had been in office for less than eighteen months following a period of thirteen years of Conservative rule. The main point at issue during the election was the country's perilous economic position, which Labour claimed was the result of a prolonged period of Tory misrule, while the latter attributed it to the mismanagement of the new Labour government.

The Labour Party claimed that it was taking decisions, however painful, that the Conservatives had shirked, and emphasized its confidence that its leading figures had considerably enhanced their reputations since becoming ministers by its use of the slogan "You *Know* Labour Government Works." The Conservatives retaliated by suggesting that the Labour government had been more productive of promises than of deeds and chose as its slogan "Action not Words."

The major political exchanges during elections now take place on the television screen. The 1959 election was the first of which this was really true, as in previous elections only a minority of voters had access to a television set. But the trend had become increasingly apparent ever since the first television election broadcasts, watched by less than 10 per cent of the electorate, were screened in 1951. By 1959 75 per cent of households possessed television sets and by 1966 this figure had risen to 88 per cent (which meant that 92 per cent of *people* had access to television sets[2]).

Television election broadcasts consist of two kinds: those for which parties are responsible and news and other broadcasts undertaken by the BBC and the various commercial companies. The party broadcasts—for which the broadcasting authorities make time available without financial charge—have been transmitted at each election since 1951, but those for which the broadcasting companies were responsible date from the 1959 general election.

Party political broadcasts in this form are a distinctively British phenomenon. In addition to those which take place during election campaigns, facilities are provided for their regular presentation during the periods between elections. For instance, during 1967 the Labour and Conservative parties were allocated five television broadcasts each, totalling sixty minutes, the Liberals two broadcasts totalling twenty minutes and the Scottish and Welsh Nationalists one five-minute broadcast each (broadcast only in Scotland and Wales respectively). The allocation of time for these broadcasts is made at an annual meeting between spokesmen of the three main

[2] Information made available by the British Broadcasting Corporation and the Independent Television Authority.

parties and representatives of the BBC and ITA. The support secured by parties at the previous general election is taken as the general basis for determining the relative amount of broadcasting time they should have.

The series of party political broadcasts held during an election campaign are similarly arranged at a meeting or meetings between the same participants. The criterion for the apportionment of time is the number of candidates in the field at the forthcoming election rather than the number of votes achieved last time. In the 1966 general election it was agreed that there should be thirteen broadcasts by the main parties. The Labour and Conservative parties had five each (two of fifteen minutes and three of ten minutes), and the Liberal Party had three (one of fifteen minutes and two of ten minutes).

There was one regional broadcast of five minutes each for the Scottish and Welsh Nationalists, and it was agreed that any other party which nominated fifty candidates or more should have a single national broadcast of five minutes. The only party to qualify under this rule was the Communist Party.

Representatives of the minor parties are excluded from the meetings agreeing the allocation of broadcasting time, and until 1965 neither the Scottish nor the Welsh Nationalists received any time at all. The Communist Party is particularly bitter at its exclusion and has more than once alleged that the Chief Whips of the three large parties "have carved up the time among themselves."

The programmes are normally produced by the BBC and made available to Independent Television, though occasionally one of the independent companies is in charge of production. In the course of production the BBC watches points of broadcasting or legal policy—an appeal for monetary contributions would be disallowed, for example, as well as any libellous content. Otherwise, in all political respects the content is the sole responsibility of the party concerned. The programmes are relayed simultaneously on all three television channels.

The use which the parties have made of their television programmes has varied considerably, and none of them has stuck to a consistent style throughout the five general elections in which television broadcasts have taken place. A wide variety of techniques has been adopted—live talks delivered straight into the camera by party leaders, filmed interviews—sometimes conducted by hostile journalists, sometimes by friendly MPs, interviews with voters in the street, specially shot film sequences, newsreel material and a great many charts, graphs and animated cartoons. The parties showed great hesitancy in deciding whether to build their programmes round the most senior party spokesmen or to make use of their more experienced television performers, most of whom are lower down in the party hierarchy. By 1959 all parties appeared to have come round to the view that the actual party leader, whose significance to the electorate as an actual or potential prime minister could scarcely be exaggerated, must have the lion's share of the available time, and since that time the final broadcast of each party has been reserved for a direct appeal to the voters by the leader.

The professional standard of party television broadcasts has gradually improved over the years, but a perceptive comment by Martin Harrison on the 1966 election series indicates that many producers and performers have still a great deal to learn about effective broadcasting techniques—"Learning from criticism and changed conditions, the major parties had abandoned complicated gimmickry in favour of a direct, almost austere style. Yet some old faults remained—notably the tendency to overload the programmes with too many speakers, too many points and too many changes of pace. Over-compression frequently led to stilted scripts which defied natural delivery. More than one broadcast became a procession of performers reciting lifeless prose with eyes glazed through excessive rehearsal or preoccupation with the 'Auto-cue.' Perhaps it is asking too much to expect politicians to be able to switch abruptly from partisan harangues on the hustings to the wholly different style and tone required for a televised talk to a family by their fireside. The Liberals, nevertheless, did grasp the need to hold their audiences, to put over a limited number of points, and to back arguments with evidence rather than *ex cathedra* assertions. Yet while Labour and the Conservatives still often lacked respect for the medium and ignored basic communication skills, in their differing ways Mr Wilson, Mr Gollan [the Communist leader] and Mr Heath in his final broadcast all showed they could use television effectively."[3]

The election programmes staged by the BBC and the commercial television companies have been hindered, on the one hand by an understandable desire to do nothing which would offend any of the party authorities, and on the other by serious doubts as to the legal standing of such broadcasts. The Representation of the People Act of 1949 had laid down that any operation "presenting the candidate or his views" should be chargeable to election expenses. Newspapers were specifically excluded from this provision, but no mention was made of radio or television.[4] The television companies were also

[3] From *The British General Election of 1966, op cit.*, p. 141.

[4] See pp. 160–1, below.

bound by the Television Act of 1954 which prohibited political broadcasting, other than party political broadcasts, unless it was in the form of "properly balanced discussion or debates."

These legal barriers partly account for the extreme timidity shown by the broadcasting authorities in the period before 1959. At no previous general election had they screened any programmes with a political content and their handling of election news items had been extremely circumspect. The Rochdale by-election in 1958, when the Granada network screened a programme in which all three candidates appeared, marked a new departure. By 1959, fortified by legal advice, both television services had resolved to take the plunge and to embark on their own election programmes.

The most notable of these, in 1959, were the BBC's "Hustings" and Granada's "Election Marathon." In the former series, two of which were produced in each of six of the BBC's seven regions, selected candidates from each of the three parties answered questions from an invited audience made up of supporters of each party. In the Welsh service programmes a candidate representing Plaid Cymru also took part.

"Election Marathon" was intended to consist of very short speeches, presented at off-peak viewing hours, by all the candidates in the area (in the north of England) covered by the Granada network. In fact, of the 348 candidates eligible to take part only 231 appeared, as a number refused and Granada took the view that if one candidate in a constituency declined to take part his opponents also must be barred from the screen.

More important than the election programmes sponsored by the television authorities, was the fact that for the first time full news coverage was given to the election. Several times every day newsreel extracts from the speeches of party leaders appeared on the screen and every effort was made to give a balanced and comprehensive account of the progress of the campaign.

The absence of accusations of partisanship and the high viewing figures obtained by political programmes in the 1959 election encouraged the television authorities to be much bolder in their coverage of subsequent elections. A judgment by the Electoral Court in December 1964 has resulted in a further lessening of their inhibitions concerning electoral broadcasts.

The circumstances of this judgment are worth recalling. In the 1964 general election the Communist Party nominated a candidate in Kinross and West Perthshire, the constituency represented by the then Prime Minister, Sir Alec Douglas-Home. Their avowed object in doing so was to claim equal broadcasting time for their nominee.

The Communist claim for time was rejected, and after the election their candidate petitioned the Court to declare Sir Alec's election void, alleging that expenditure on party broadcasts by the BBC and ITA was improperly incurred "with a view to promoting the election of a candidate." The Court held that though Sir Alec may incidentally have gained some personal electoral advantage from the broadcasts, the "dominant motive" of the BBC and ITA was "to give information to the public and not to promote the election of the respondents." It therefore refused the Communists' petition.[5]

Following this judgment, the broadcasting authorities have felt free to continue to present programmes in which candidates appear as spokesmen for their parties, so long as no reference is made to the campaign in their own constituencies. But in programmes specifically concerned with constituency campaigns, including those during Parliamentary by-elections, the rule is scrupulously adhered to that no candidate may appear unless all his opponents are included in the same programme.

In 1966 the election campaign was very fully reported in the news bulletins, and each broadcasting authority ran a daily campaign report and a wide variety of special programmes on the election. At no British general election so far has there been a direct confrontation between the party leaders on the lines of the Kennedy–Nixon debates in 1960. In 1964 Harold Wilson, who was then Leader of the Opposition, proposed such a programme, but Sir Alec Douglas-Home was unwilling to appear. In 1966 both Harold Wilson and Edward Heath agreed in principle, but it proved impossible to produce mutually acceptable conditions.

The nearest substitute to a debate between the party leaders has been the "Election Forum" series run by the BBC in both 1964 and 1966. In these the three party leaders have appeared on successive nights and have answered questions submitted by viewers and put by a panel of TV interviewers. These programmes have attracted a great deal of public interest—18,000 questions were sent in by viewers in 1964 and 12,000 in 1966. The size of audiences which they attracted was also impressive—in 1966 Mr Wilson was watched by over ten million viewers, Mr Heath by over eight million and Mr Grimond by seven million.

The audiences for the party election broadcasts were even higher, but as these were broadcast simultaneously on all three channels a fair proportion of them must have been "captive" viewers. Indeed, there is a growing feeling that with the new freedom for broad-

[5] See *The Times*, London, December 22, 23, 24, 1964 for a full report of this case.

casting authorities to present programmes of this type, the party political broadcast has outlived its usefulness. Certainly, both the BBC and ITA would be happy to dispense with them—or at least those held between election campaigns—but so far the political parties have been reluctant to give them up. No doubt they regard them as a valuable asset—one writer has calculated that in the 1964 campaign and in the period of two years leading up to it the commercial value of the free time allocated to each major party was approximately £3 million.[6]

There is much evidence that television has enabled voters in general elections to be better informed on the issues and to be more familiar with the personalities of leading politicians than ever before.[7] It has often been observed that television has enabled a modern political leader to speak to more people in one evening than the total number that Gladstone or Disraeli succeeded in addressing at all the meetings during their entire careers. In 1966 more than eight voters out of ten heard one or more of the party political broadcasts and virtually 100 per cent must have heard some extracts from election speeches on television or radio news bulletins. This is a far higher proportion than has ever been reached through constituency campaigning.

Television has also had its effects on other aspects of electioneering. The reporting of speeches in news bulletins enables rival political leaders to reply to each others' charges several times during the course of a day and thus the whole tempo of campaigning has been speeded up. Television has greatly increased the exposure of partisans to the propaganda of the other side and this has almost certainly led to greater sophistication in the propaganda of all parties. It has also resulted in less partisanship in the Press, as radio and television programmes are widely and justifiably regarded as impartial, and are thus used as a yardstick against which newspaper reports may be measured.

The arrangements for sound broadcasting are similar to those for television. The political parties are allocated time according to the same formula, and the BBC (which has a monopoly of sound broadcasting) produces its own programmes on the election and provides full news coverage. Sound radio played a more important role in the period before the development and diffusion of television, but

[6] See Richard Rose, *op. cit.*, p. 205.

[7] See Joseph Trenaman and Denis McQuail, *Television and the Political Image* (London, Methuen, 1961) for a detailed account of the effects of television in the 1959 election. No major study has yet been published of television in elections subsequent to 1959.

it now caters most of the time for only a minority audience—though one which is still large by any standard other than that set by TV. The first election broadcasts on sound radio were in 1924, but it was in the elections of the 'thirties, 'forties and early 'fifties that the "wireless" had its most significant effect on elections. Now its main importance is as a purveyor of news, especially at breakfast time when the television receivers are silent.

The role of the Press in general elections, while still important, is shrinking. Television and radio are regarded both as more impartial and more immediate sources of election news, while opinion polls have largely robbed newspapers of their claim to represent public opinion. None the less, all newspapers continue to devote extensive space to covering elections and each in its own distinctive way attempts to persuade its readers to support the party of its choice.

The degree of partisanship displayed by newspapers and the consistency with which they support a political party vary considerably, but on the evidence of their current editorial policies and their record at recent general elections, the political affiliations of national daily newspapers can be spelled out with reasonable certainty. The present line-up, with the most recently available circulation figures (those for the period January–June 1966) is shown in Table 16.

Table 16—Circulations of National Newspapers, June 1966

Conservative		*Labour*	
Daily Express	3,953,612	*Daily Mirror*	5,077,548
Daily Mail	2,381,223	*The Sun*	1,247,818
Daily Telegraph	1,354,146	*The Guardian*	282,709
Daily Sketch	849,396		
Total	8,538,377		6,608,075

The Guardian is, traditionally, a Liberal newspaper and still gives a measure of support to that party, but in recent years it has moved rather nearer to the Labour Party. *The Times* (circulation 273,148) has tended to offer lukewarm support to the Conservatives, but in 1966 it expressed a rather muddled neutrality. The Liberal Party has had no consistent supporter since 1960 when the *News Chronicle* (circulation 1,100,000) closed down, while the Communist *Morning Star* (formerly *Daily Worker*) enjoys only a minuscule circulation. Labour lost its firmest supporter in 1964 when the *Daily Herald* (in which the Trades Union Congress held a minority share-holding) was replaced by *The Sun*, wholly owned by Mr Cecil King's International Publishing Corporation. While professing political independence, *The Sun* has continued to support Labour, but commercial success has so far eluded it and its publication beyond 1968 is in some doubt.

The various morning, daily and evening papers published outside London are much more uniformly pro-Conservative than is the national Press. But, dependent as they are on sales to people of all political views within the area in which they are published, they tend to be less partison in style. The majority of them give reasonably full coverage during and between elections to the activities and viewpoints of the anti-Conservative parties.

The influence which the Press has on its readers' voting intentions is slight, and is probably stronger between elections than during the actual campaign. In fact the majority of voters read newspapers with which they are politically in agreement, so the scope for effecting conversions is limited. Among national newspapers, only the *Daily Express* and, to a lesser extent the *Daily Mirror*, enjoy a large readership amongst their political opponents.

It has been suggested by some authorities that the *Daily Mirror* alone of British newspapers had a significant influence on voting in recent years. Thus, the Labour victory in 1945 was partly attributed to a *Mirror* feature entitled "Vote for them," in which wives, mothers and sweethearts of servicemen overseas were entreated to vote Labour for their absent loved ones. Again, in 1951, the *Daily Mirror* headline "Whose finger on the trigger?" was supposed to have robbed the Conservatives of a more pronounced victory by suggesting, at the height of the Abadan crisis, that a Conservative prime minister was more likely to precipitate a war. It now seems probable that the influence of the *Daily Mirror* was grossly exaggerated on both occasions.[8] Though newspapers remain a major source of election news and take a lively part in the campaign, all the evidence suggests their influence on the results is extremely limited.

The parties are nevertheless anxious to secure as much publicity in the Press, as well as on television and radio, as possible. In the 1959 campaign the then general secretary of the Labour Party, Morgan Phillips, held daily Press conferences which proved so newsworthy that the Labour campaign threatened at one time almost to monopolize space in the most Conservative of newspapers. A week later the Conservatives retaliated and Lord Hailsham (Quintin Hogg) and Lord Poole, their then chairman and vice-chairman, met the Press each day at a similar function.

[8] For a too flattering assessment of the influence of the *Daily Mirror* in the post-war period see Maurice Edelman, *The Mirror; A Political History* (London, Hamish Hamilton, 1966).

Since then the daily Press conferences have played a leading role in each party's campaign, and, indeed, Harold Wilson in 1964 and Edward Heath in 1966 chose to conduct their parties' conferences themselves, as their main contribution to the electoral campaign.

An important feature until very recently was the speaking tours undertaken by the party leaders, who would roam the country speaking to a large number of meetings, some of them in the open-air, in support of their party's candidates. In 1959, for instance, Harold Macmillan in a sixteen-day tour made seventy-four speeches while Hugh Gaitskell made fifty-three speeches in thirteen days. Since then, however, the leaders have preferred to remain in London, exercising a close supervision over the central direction of the campaign, and have tended to restrict their platform appearances to major evening meetings from which they usually return to London the same night. In 1966 the "whistle stop" tours were assigned to the respective deputy leaders, George Brown and Reginald Maudling.

Apart from their publicity value, which is great, visits by party leaders put great heart into their supporters wherever they go. Large crowds are almost invariably attracted, far larger than for other political gatherings. A visit by the party leader early in the campaign can give a tremendous fillip to a local party and help to attract a large number of volunteers to help in the campaign.

The role of party leaders in election campaigns varies both according to their personalities and whether they are in government or opposition. A greater effort is normally expected from the Leader of the Opposition, who can be expected to put all his energy into campaigning, while the Prime Minister has concurrently to concern himself with the government of the country. Even as energetic a man as Harold Wilson fought a markedly less strenuous campaign in 1966 than he had, as opposition leader, in 1964.

As the campaign draws to a close, the party leaders finally set off for their own constituencies with a sense of profound relief.

The extreme exertion of the preceding three weeks are over, and there is now no more that they can do to influence the result. Their absence from their constituencies during the greater part of the campaign is unlikely to have caused any undue concern, for party leaders normally represent safe seats. During the last one or two days before the votes are cast they occupy themselves in much the same way as other candidates, but with the knowledge that they will soon be set apart from them, either to taste the power and responsibility of the premiership or to assume the scarcely less onerous, but infinitely less rewarding, responsibility of leading their parties on the opposition benches of the House of Commons.

10. Polling Day

WHEN POLLING DAY FINALLY ARRIVES THE LIMELIGHT WHICH HAS shone throughout the preceding weeks on the party leaders and the national campaigns of the parties swings decisively back to the constituencies. The morning papers carry final appeals to vote for one or other of the parties, but otherwise an uneasy quiet descends upon the national scene. The final shots have been fired on radio and television, the party headquarters have done their best or their worst, all now depends on the voter.

Polling day is a very long one for those most intimately concerned. The earliest risers are the presiding officers and poll clerks of the various polling stations. They have to be at their posts by 6.30 a.m., or thereabouts, in order to be ready to receive the first voters at seven o'clock.

Each polling station is in charge of a presiding officer, who has a number of poll clerks to help him. Most polling stations are housed in schools, but a wide variety of other premises are used in some constituencies. If no suitable building is available, a temporary prefabricated building may be erected for the occasion. On arrival at the polling station, the presiding officer has to satisfy himself that all the necessary equipment has been installed.

Inside the polling station will be a row of voting compartments, shaped like telephone kiosks, but with a sliding curtain covering the entrance to ensure privacy. Within the compartment will be a shelf, at waist height, on which voters can mark their ballot papers. A strong indelible pencil is attached by string to the shelf. A notice giving instructions how to vote is pinned up in each voting compartment, and is also displayed outside the polling station.

Opposite the voting compartments is a table or tables behind which the presiding officer and his assistants sit. In between, in full view of the presiding officer, stand one or more ballot boxes. The presiding officer will have been supplied with a copy of the election register for his polling district, a list of proxy and postal voters, an adequate supply of ballot papers and equipment for marking the ballot papers with the official mark. The ballot papers are printed in books, with counterfoils, rather like cloakroom tickets. Serial numbers are printed on the back of each paper and each counterfoil.

The presiding officer is in sole charge of his polling station. He and his assistants have to swear a declaration of secrecy that they will not divulge, except for some purpose authorized by law, any information as to who has or has not voted or reveal to anyone before the close of the poll the nature of the official mark. A similar declaration has to be made by the candidate and his agent or representatives before they may be admitted to a polling station for any purpose except to cast their own votes.

It is the responsibility of the presiding officer to see that no unauthorized person is admitted to the polling station, that order is maintained and that the poll is conducted lawfully in every respect. At least one police constable will be on duty throughout the day at each polling station to assist the presiding officer to keep order.

Immediately before the poll opens at seven o'clock, the presiding officer must show the ballot box empty to whoever is in the polling station and then lock it and place his seal on the lock.

When the first voter arrives he will give his full name and address to the polling clerk who will tell him his number, put a tick against his name on the register, write his electoral number on the counterfoil of the ballot paper, emboss the ballot paper with the official mark and hand the ballot paper to the voter. The purpose of the official mark, the nature of which is kept secret, is to prevent the forgery of ballot papers. Poll clerks must take great care to remember to emboss each paper as it is issued, or the vote will later be invalidated through no fault of the voter.[1] It is improper to emboss ballot papers in advance, because of the risk of theft.

The voter takes his ballot paper into one of the voting compartments and marks an X against the candidate of his choice. There is no indication on the ballot paper of the party of the candidates,[2] nor may the voter enquire this information of the presiding officer or poll clerks. Though the great majority of voters, will have learnt before reaching the polling station who represents whom, a handful of voters in each constituency are uncertain and confused and consequently find themselves voting by accident against the party of their choice.

All that the ballot papers do contain are the surnames of the

[1] In Derbyshire North-East, in 1922, the Labour candidate was elected by 5 votes, with a larger number of unmarked ballot papers in favour of his opponent. It is clear that he owed his victory to the failure of the poll clerks to mark some of the ballot papers.

[2] See page 128, below.

candidates, in alphabetical order, and their full names and addresses and descriptions, which normally refers to their occupation. A sample ballot paper is shown in Figure 6.

When he has marked his ballot paper the voter must fold it, and, in the view of the presiding officer, drop it into the ballot box. By this elaborate procedure the secrecy of the ballot is at once protected and the possibility of forged papers being introduced into the ballot box virtually eliminated.

Figure 6—Sample Ballot Paper

SMITH (James Henry Smith of 27 Roundchurch Mansions, London, S.E.22, Plumber.)	
TAYLOR (William Thomas Percy Taylor of "Littlehammer," Abinger, Surrey, Company Director.)	
YOUNG (Mary Jane Young of 14 Argyll Road, Oldham, Lancashire, Housewife.)	

If a voter spoils his ballot paper he may obtain another one on application to the presiding officer, who will mark the spoiled paper "cancelled" and put it on one side till the end of the day, when he has to account to the Returning Officer for all the ballot papers which he has issued.

Blind and incapacitated voters may ask the presiding officer to mark their ballot papers for them, or may bring a friend with them who will be permitted to mark their ballot papers for them.

If the election is on a Saturday, which does not normally happen in the case of Parliamentary elections though many local government elections are held on that day, a Jewish voter who objects on religious grounds to voting in the prescribed manner may also request the presiding officer to mark his ballot paper for him.

By the time the first voters have cast their votes, the election agent and his helpers will already be in action. Outside each polling station will be "tellers," each proudly sporting his party colours, who will ask voters for their electoral numbers as they leave the polling stations. There is no obligation on voters to reveal this information but the great majority of them are normally willing to do so, at least to the tellers representing their own party. Many of the tellers are school-children who are on holiday for the day and have been recruited for the job by parents who are staunch party members. Sometimes they may be paid by the party or their parents, but most of them are willing to help out for nothing. An excess of zeal may occasionally be revealed in a frosty unwillingness to co-operate with the tellers from "the other side," but more frequently a feeling of *camaraderie* prevails and numbers are willingly swopped.

Tellers also represent the last resource of parties to remind voters of the names of their candidates, and it is fairly common for an absent-minded voter to check with his party's teller on his way into the polling station the name of the person for whom he should vote.

Each party will have established a sub-committee room near to the polling station which will contain a copy of the register on which will be marked all the voters who have promised to support the party's candidate. At hourly intervals, or possibly more frequently, throughout the day messengers will bring back from the tellers lists of the electoral numbers of those who have already voted so that they can be crossed off the register. An army of "knockers up" will have been recruited to call later in the day on those who have not already voted.

Soon after breakfast the candidate, wearing an outsize rosette, will be ceremoniously introduced—probably by his agent—to the presiding officer, with whom he will exchange a few light-hearted remarks. The ostensible reason for the visit is to satisfy himself that everything is in order, though there is virtually never any question of this not being the case. During his tour the candidate will also drop into all his sub-committee rooms to give a word of encouragement to his supporters.

Throughout the day his party is likely to have one or more loudspeaker cars touring areas where its support is concentrated, urging voters to record their votes as early as possible in the day, thus reducing the pressure on the party machine during the evening. For much of the day the candidate himself is likely to be in charge of the loudspeaker, making a personal appeal to the voters to support him.

By 9 a.m. perhaps one elector in ten may have voted. The

majority of these would be men, casting their votes on their way to work. During the daytime a steady trickle of housewives make their way to the polling stations, but a surprisingly high proportion prefer to wait until the evening and to go along with their husbands.

The result is that many party workers find themselves less than fully occupied until at least five or six o'clock in the evening. In the morning and afternoon sick and elderly voters are called on and offered lifts to the poll. Knockers up will be kept busy throughout the afternoon, but will find many houses empty and at others will be told to come back in the evening.

By six o'clock it is unusual for more than 50 per cent of the electors to have cast their votes and about that time begins an increasingly frantic effort by each party machine to get its supporters to the poll in the three hours remaining. This is especially important for the Labour Party, as working-class wives are much less likely to vote earlier in the day than their middle-class counterparts. A much higher proportion of Labour votes than of Conservative ones are cast in the evening, and non-political factors such as the weather and the appeal of the evening's television programmes can have an important effect on the result in closely contested constituencies.

In the evening every available helper is mobilized to knock up voters and, wherever possible, a car is provided for every group of knockers up, so that lifts to the poll may be offered to reluctant voters. Parties with a good and well-manned organization may well be able to knock up all their supporters who have not voted earlier, as many as six times during the course of the evening. Despite this encouragement some voters remain obdurate and refuse to turn out, others delay so long that in the end it is too late to go, a few arrive at the polling station after nine o'clock and find it closed.

But allowing for inaccuracies in the election register, for removals and for people who are sick or away from their homes on election day, without having arranged to vote by post, the proportion of electors who actually vote in Parliamentary elections is rather high. Since 1950 it has ranged from 75·2 per cent to 84·0 per cent, which suggests that the proportion of avoidable abstentions is probably not usually much more than 10 per cent.

Promptly at 9 p.m., the presiding officer must close his polling station, even if there are electors waiting to cast their votes. He must then seal the ballot boxes, so that no more ballot papers may be inserted. He then makes out his ballot paper account. On this he must state the number of ballot papers with which he had been issued at the beginning of the day, the number of papers in the ballot box and the number of unused and spoilt papers. He must then make up packages containing the marked registers, the counterfoils and the unused ballot papers and deliver these to the returning officer. The police, under the direction of the returning officer, will collect the ballot boxes and take them straight to the place where the votes are to be counted.

The count is usually held in the town hall or other large public hall in the constituency. In nearly all borough constituencies it is held on the evening of polling day; in most counties it is postponed until the following morning. It is a crowded and lively occasion. The hall is furnished with long trestle tables at either side of which are seated the returning officer's assistants who are to count the votes. There is an air of expectancy as the room gradually fills up with candidates, their wives, agents and leading supporters, whose function is to act as "counting agents" or scrutineers of the actual counting of the votes. The number of counting agents permitted to each candidate is decided by the returning officer, but the total should not be less than the number of counting assistants and each candidate must be allowed the same number. All attending the count must sign a declaration of secrecy, promising not to attempt to discover how any individual has voted or to reveal such information to any other person. The Press may be admitted, at the discretion of the returning officer, and a public gallery may also be provided.

By about 9.15 p.m. in most boroughs the first ballot boxes will arrive from the polling stations. The ballot box containing the postal votes will be among the first to arrive.

Each box is emptied of its contents, which are immediately counted to make sure that they tally with the number given in the presiding officer's ballot paper account. When every box has been emptied and its contents counted the ballot papers are mixed together in one large pile, so that it is impossible to tell accurately how the voters of each polling district have recorded their votes.

The ballot papers are now sorted out into piles representing votes polled for each individual candidate. They are then counted into bundles of one hundred. All the time the counting agents, who will be standing behind the counting assistants, will be keeping an eagle eye on their activities—making sure that none of their candidate's papers have inadvertently been included amongst those of their opponents.

In a safe or hopeless constituency there is little tension, and the candidates and their supporters are much more concerned with whispered reports that may be coming in about the results in other constituencies, and the national trend to which they point. Some thoughtful returning officers go to the trouble of installing a television set in an anteroom and many scrutineers spend a lot of their time popping in and out to acquaint themselves with the latest position.

In a marginal constituency, however, attention is firmly fixed on the counting, and as the rival piles of votes mount so do the hopes and fears of the candidates and their supporters.

In the process of sorting the votes the counting assistants come across a number of ballot papers whose validity is doubtful. They place these on one side and when all the other votes have been counted the returning officer adjudicates them in the presence of the candidates and their agents, giving his reasons for accepting, or rejecting, them in each case.

There are four categories of ballot paper which must be declared void—those which do not bear the official mark, those on which votes are given for more than one candidate, those on which anything is written by which the voter can be identified and those which are unmarked.

Other papers in which the intention of the voter is unclear should be declared invalid by the returning officer, but where the intention is clear, but the mark has been incorrectly made he should accept their validity. Examples of incorrectly marked papers which are nevertheless valid are those where the X is placed otherwise than in the proper place, but still leaving no doubt which candidate the voter prefers; those where a tick or similar mark has been used instead of a cross and those where "Yes" and "No," or "1" and "2" or "1" and "0" have been written to express a preference between candidates.

When the returning officer has given his adjudication of the doubtful votes they should be added to their appropriate pile and the total of each candidate's votes will be recorded by the chief counting assistant who will give it to the returning officer. The returning officer will then privately inform the candidates and their agents of the result of the count. If the result is close the returning officer may order a recount, and any candidate may claim a recount which the returning officer may not reasonably refuse. If the first count shows a majority of less than 500 a demand for a recount is likely, and where the majority is less than a hundred several recounts may be held. It is also permissible for a recount to be demanded by a candidate in danger of losing his deposit where the number of his votes is close to the minimum required, even though the majority of the leading candidate may be numbered in tens of thousands.

If after several recounts, there is an equality of votes between the two leading candidates, the returning officer draws a lot to decide which is elected. Prior to 1948 the rule was that the returning officer should have a casting vote. The last occasion on which this invidious situation arose in Parliamentary elections was at Ashton-under-Lyne in 1886, but there have been a number of more recent examples in local government elections.

As soon as the result of the poll has been ascertained, the returning officer makes a public announcement of the votes obtained by the various candidates and declares the new Member elected. It is then usual for the winning candidate to propose a vote of thanks to the returning officer and his staff for their conduct of the election, during which he takes the opportunity of thanking his own supporters and declaring that the result is a triumph for his party and the cause which it represents. The vote of thanks is seconded by the runner-up, who also gives his own partisan interpretation of the result, as do other candidates (if any) who are also expected to have their say. Great demonstrations of enthusiasm are made by their supporters, especially by the winning party when the seat has changed hands.

As soon as possible after the result has been declared, the returning officer must publish it in writing. He must also attach, to the writ which he has received from the Clerk of the Crown authorizing him to conduct the election, a certificate naming the newly elected Member. The writ is then returned, post free, to the Clerk of the Crown.

The returning officer must also collect up all the documents concerned with the election—the ballot papers used and unused, the ballot paper accounts and rejected ballot papers, the marked copies of the election registers and lists of proxies and the counterfoils of all ballot papers—and send these to the Clerk of the Crown. All these documents will be retained for one year and then destroyed, unless an order to the contrary is made by the High Court or the House of Commons.

The validity of an election may be challenged by a petition to the High Court, which may be presented by an elector for the constituency concerned or by one of the candidates. The Court, in considering the petition, may order a scrutiny of the ballot papers and other relevant documents listed above. The High Court must report its findings to the Speaker of the House of Commons and if it has found the election invalid the House will proceed to authorize the issue of a writ for a new election.

Election petitions are rare, partly no doubt because of the great expense involved to the petitioner and partly because a Member is unlikely to be unseated if only minor irregularities are proved.[3] The most recent election petition was that against Sir Alec Douglas-Home, in 1964, mentioned on page 103. But the only one in recent years alleging irregularity in the actual constituency campaign was that brought by Sir Oswald Mosley following his defeat as a Union Movement candidate at North Kensington in 1959. It was unsuccessful, as was that concerning the Drake division of Plymouth in 1929, the only other petition to be made, since 1924, except those concerning Mr Wedgwood Benn and the two Sinn Fein Members in Northern Ireland, discussed on page 66. In each of these three cases the issue was the qualification of the candidates not the conduct of the election. But the main reason why election petitions are seldom resorted to is the undoubted fact that major irregularities are almost unknown in modern British elections.

On election night special programmes relaying the constituency results as they become known are broadcast on sound radio and both television channels. Expert commentators interpret the results and, on the basis of the trend revealed by the first contests to be counted, attempt, usually with a large measure of success, to predict what the final result will be. Electronic computers, which have been used for the same purpose, have not noticeably improved on the accuracy of their predictions.[4]

There is lively competition to be the first constituency to declare a result. Traditionally, the city of Salford which contains two constituencies has claimed this honour, but in 1959 it was pipped at the post by Billericay, while in both 1964 and 1966 Cheltenham was the first result to be declared. But any constituency which consists of a highly concentrated urban area stands a good chance of being first, so long as its returning officer is prepared to spend extra money on employing more numerous and better skilled counting assistants—and unless, of course, there is a recount.

Normally, the first result is available by ten o'clock and by 4 a.m.

[3] Butler and Rose, *The British General Election of 1959* (London, Macmillan, 1960), p. 280, quote a senior party organizer on this point: "If we lost a seat by one vote and I could clearly prove illegal practices by the other side I wouldn't try. It would cost perhaps £5,000 and they might be able to show that our man had slipped up in some way. But worse than that, it might start tit-for-tat petitions and no party could afford a lot of them. On the whole, we are both law-abiding and it's as well to leave each other alone."

[4] It is the high degree of homogeneity of the British electorate which enables such forecasts to be made on the basis of the first handful of results.

when the broadcasting programmes close down for the night over 450 constituencies will have been counted. By this time the result of the election should be clear, unless it is extremely close. As it is, predominantly, the urban seats which are counted overnight, Labour needs to establish a considerable lead among these if it is to emerge as the final victor. A Labour lead of less than fifty overnight points to a Conservative victory while if the figures show Labour between fifty and sixty-five seats ahead it is certain that the result will be close.

At about ten o'clock the following day the count is begun in the other constituencies and from eleven o'clock onwards the results are broadcast, as they come in, to about 6 p.m., by which time all but a handful of remote Scottish constituencies have declared their results. Long before this one of the party leaders will normally have conceded defeat, and it will be clear who is to govern the country for the next four or five years.

11. By-Elections and Local Elections

CASUAL VACANCIES IN THE HOUSE OF COMMONS ARE FILLED THROUGH by-elections in the constituency concerned. Such vacancies may be occasioned by the death, succession or elevation to the peerage, bankruptcy, lunacy, expulsion from the House or the acceptance of a disqualifying office by a Member of Parliament. There is no formal provision for a Member to resign his seat, but resignation is effected by applying for a disqualifying office. Two such offices—sinecures of great antiquity—are normally reserved for such a purpose—the posts of Steward of the Chiltern Hundreds and Bailiff of the Manor of Northstead.

In practice, the great majority of by-elections are caused by deaths, resignations or elevation to the peerage. Table 17 shows the number of by-elections held during each Parliament since 1945, and the reasons for them. During the whole period there has, on average, been 11·5 by-elections per year, or just under one a month.

Table 17—By-elections 1945–66

		Caused by				
Parliament	*No. of By-elections*	*Death*	*Resignation*	*Peerage*	*Expulsion*	*Disqualification*
1945–50	52	N.A.	N.A.	N.A.	N.A.	N.A.
1950–51	16	8	7	1	—	—
1951–55	48	18	18	11	1	—
1955–59	52	25	11	14	—	2
1959–64	62	27	18	17	—	—
1964–66	13	5	2	6	—	—

N.A.=Not available

In place of the Royal Proclamation authorizing a general election, the Speaker of the House of Commons issues a writ instructing the returning officer in the constituency concerned to make arrangements for the poll to be held. Polling day is fixed between two and three weeks after the receipt of the writ (see timetable in Appendix 5). The writ is issued following a motion approved by the House of Commons, but when the House is in recess the Speaker may issue the writ on receipt of a certificate signed by any two Members of

Parliament, provided that the vacancy is caused by death or accession to the peerage.

By tradition, the party holding the seat chooses the date on which the by-election is held, and it is the party whips who move the appropriate motion in the House, which is normally agreed without discussion. Tactical considerations clearly influence the choice of date, but if it is unduly postponed there is likely to be an adverse reaction within the constituency and the opposing parties will seek to capitalize on the unwillingness of the defending party to face a contest. Most by-elections are held within three to four months of the vacancy arising, though a delay of up to six months is by no means unusual. The minimum period before a vacancy is filled is about six weeks. With very minor variations,[1] the legal provisions concerning a by-election (including the restriction on expenditure by candidates) are the same as in a general election.

Although a by-election campaign closely resembles that within an individual constituency at a general election, it frequently excites a great deal more interest. There is normally far stronger competition to be selected as a candidate, even for the minority party in a hopeless seat, as the publicity given to the by-election might well result in subsequent invitations from constituency parties in more attractive seats. At a general election an individual contest is merged in the national campaign and little note is taken of it outside the constituency concerned. At a by-election it holds the centre of the stage.

For this reason, too, it is more likely to attract intervention by minor party or independent candidates, including a few who have no serious political interests and put themselves forward purely for exhibitionist reasons. However, the likelihood of losing a deposit of £150 is a sufficient deterrent for most such people, and the majority of contests are three- or four-cornered fights. For example, a total of forty-nine candidates contested the thirteen by-elections in the Parliament of 1964–66—an average of 3·77 per contest. (In the 1966 general election 1,707 candidates contested 630 seats—an average of 2·87 per constituency.)

In fighting a by-election a constituency party can normally depend on help from outside. The party's regional organizer will probably move into the constituency for several weeks and supervise the campaign, and professional agents from other constituencies will be borrowed to undertake important specialist tasks. Other

[1] See A. Norman Schofield, *Parliamentary Elections*, Third Edition (London, Shaw and Sons, 1959), pp. 374–76.

professionals from the national party headquarters may also be seconded, while voluntary workers from neighbouring constituencies can also be expected to lend a hand. In the case of key contests in highly marginal seats helpers may travel from all parts of the country to support their party's nominee.

Traditionally, the Prime Minister sends a personal message of support to the government party's candidate, which is useful for attracting Press publicity, and the leaders of the opposition parties also send similar letters to their standard-bearers. Prominent Cabinet Ministers, and their counterparts in the other parties, descend on the constituency to speak at election meetings and MPs are drafted in to lead canvassing and loudspeaker drives.

The personality of the candidate in a by-election is more important than in a general election campaign. Freed from the awesome responsibility of helping to choose a government, voters are more prepared to cross party lines and to vote for the most attractive candidate. For the same reason, Liberals can usually hope to do rather better at by-elections. It should be stressed, however, that the difference is only *relative*. Even at by-elections the majority of voters are likely to adhere to their normal party loyalties.

Governments may appear to take by-elections more seriously than their effects would warrant. It is true that it is only rarely that a government's fate can be directed or affected by the result of a by-election. In the 1964–66 Parliament, for instance, when for most of the time the Labour Parliamentary majority was three, a loss of only two seats in by-elections would have left the government in a minority in the House of Commons and probably would have precipitated a general election at a time not of the government's choosing. But during most Parliaments the loss of six, or even a dozen, seats would still leave the government with a comfortable Parliamentary majority. Table 18 shows that in no Parliament since 1945 has any party made a net loss of more than five seats or a net gain of more than four.

Table 18—By-elections—Changes in Party Strengths

Parliament	*Total changes*	*Con.*	*Net changes* *Lab.*	*Lib.*	*Others*
1945–50	3	+3	—	—	−3
1950–51	0	—	—	—	—
1951–55	1	+1	−1	—	—
1955–59	6	−3	+4	—	−1
1959–64	7*	−5	+4	+1	—
1964–66	2	—	−1	+1	—

* Excluding two by-elections at Bristol, South East. See p. 66, above.

It may seem surprising that so few seats change hands at by-elections. One reason is that relatively few of them take place in marginal seats. Even those caused by deaths are disproportionately in safe seats, as, generally speaking, it is the younger Members who represent the more marginal seats. By-elections caused by resignations or elevation to the peerage are the consequence of voluntary decisions, and political parties seldom choose to put their marginal seats at risk, especially when they are going through a period of unpopularity.

But it is not just the *loss* of seats which governments fear. By-elections have long been used as a means of gauging public opinion, and a disappointing result, even if it does not involve the loss of a seat, can have a disastrous effect on party morale, while boosting that of the opposition. The results of by-elections can have an influence out of all proportion to their intrinsic importance, and this can best be shown by discussing briefly some of the more significant results in the post-war period.

During the Parliament of 1945–50 there was no single by-election result which had more than a passing effect. But, cumulatively, the by-elections contributed in no small measure to the standing of the then Labour Government. Although the Conservatives gained ground in the great majority of the fifty-two contests, their failure to win a single seat from Labour was constantly invoked as evidence that the government was still enjoying wide support, despite other indications to the contrary.

During the course of the 1951–55 Parliament the Conservative Government actually won a seat—Sunderland South—from the Labour Opposition. This was a rare feat indeed—the great majority of by-elections have invariably shown a swing against the government in office, and it was almost thirty years since a government had actually picked up a seat in a by-election. The consequence was that pressure on the government eased perceptibly, and most observers concluded, correctly, that the Conservatives would win the subsequent general election.

In the period from the spring of 1962 to the summer of 1964 an almost unbroken succession of by-election disasters did immense damage to the reputation of the governments of Harold Macmillan and Sir Alec Douglas-Home, and provoked them into taking a number of ill-considered actions. The most sensational result, in March 1962, was at Orpington, hitherto regarded as an extremely safe Conservative seat. The by-election resulted in a Liberal victory; a Conservative majority of 14,760 was turned into a Liberal one of 7,855. Although the Liberal revival which it appeared to foreshadow did not eventually materialize, this result largely transformed the terms in which electoral strategy was discussed. During the succeeding two years—in over thirty more by-elections—the Conservatives lost a further three seats to Labour, and suffered the further humiliation of seeing their candidate forced into third position in six Labour seats, and into fourth place in one more. The dismissal by Harold Macmillan, in July 1962, of one-third of his Cabinet, and the postponement by Sir Alec Douglas-Home of the general election until the last possible moment in 1964, were both plausibly attributed to this series of setbacks.[2]

In the 1964–66 Parliament by-elections continued to have an important influence on the fortunes of the (now Labour) Government. The completely unexpected loss of Leyton to the Conservatives in January 1965 (when a Labour majority of 7,926 was turned into a Conservative one of 205) not only led to the immediate resignation of the Foreign Secretary (Patrick Gordon Walker, who was the defeated Labour candidate), but reduced the government's precarious Parliamentary majority from five to three. It also deterred the Prime Minister from calling an early general election, which he might otherwise have been tempted to do by the favourable opinion poll findings.

A year later—in January 1966—in a keenly contested by-election at North Hull the Labour Party increased its majority from 1,181 to 5,351, obtaining a swing of 4·5 per cent—the largest swing to the governing party in any by-election in a marginal seat in thirty-two years. This result confirmed other evidence (from opinion polls) that an early general election would produce an increased Labour Parliamentary majority, and the North Hull result certainly appears to have clinched the Prime Minister's decision to go to the country in March 1966. Though the North Hull result created less of a stir than that of some other by-elections, especially Orpington, it probably had a more decisive political significance than any other by-election in the past half century.

Despite the influence which by-elections such as this undoubtedly had, there is a serious risk of reading too much into individual by-election results. In fact, the result of any particular by-election may be wildly misleading as a reflection of the national strength of the parties. Regional and local issues which tend to cancel out in a general election may assume disproportionate importance; the turnout, which at a general election is normally between 75 and 85 per

[2] Though in the latter case the public opinion poll trends, which fully confirmed the adverse by-election results, were probably equally responsible.

cent, fluctuates widely (in the 1955–59 Parliament, for instance, from 24·9 to 90·4 per cent); the personal qualities of candidates have a greater effect than in a general election; and minor party and independent candidates are more likely to intervene and their influence, though marginal, is difficult to interpret.

The fallacy of drawing too many conclusions from the result of a single by-election can easily be illustrated. In November 1960 six by-elections were fought on the same day. In one of these, Carshalton, there was a swing to the Conservatives of 3·8 per cent; in another, Bolton East, there was a swing to Labour of 2·0 per cent—a difference of 5·8 per cent. Similarly, in May 1964, by-elections held on the same day at Devizes and Winchester showed pro-Labour swings of 2·8 per cent and 8·6 per cent respectively—again a difference of 5·8 per cent.

Single by-election results, then, are clearly unreliable guides to the state of public opinion, but experience has shown that groups of by-elections, held over a period of several months, do give a reasonably accurate idea of the *trend* of opinion, if their results are averaged out. Figure 7[3] shows the results of all the by-elections between 1945 and 1966, averaged out at quarterly periods. It bears a close resemblance to Figure 8, on page 145, which traces the result of Gallup poll findings in the same period. It also demonstrates very clearly that the great majority of by-elections show a swing against the government in power.

The reasons for this can only be conjectured, but it seems probable that by-elections are often used as a means of registering a "protest vote" against particular government policies, without incurring the risk of actually overthrowing the government. The turnout at by-elections is almost invariably lower than at a general election,[4] and it may also be the case that government supporters are rather more inclined to be complacent, and to stay at home on such occasions.

In any event, Table 19[5] clearly shows that at every general election since the war the governing party has done better than the previous by-election results had indicated. Over the twenty-one years between 1945 and 1966 by-election swings have shown an average bias of 3·1 per cent against the party in office.

[3] Reproduced from *The Gallup Election Handbook 1966* (London, Gallup Poll, 1966), p. 25.

[4] For instance, the turn-out in the 13 by-elections in the 1964–66 Parliament was, on average, 64.4 per cent. In the 1964 general election it was 77.0 per cent, and in 1966, 75.8 per cent.

[5] Adapted from *The Gallup Election Handbook 1966*, *op. cit.*, p. 26.

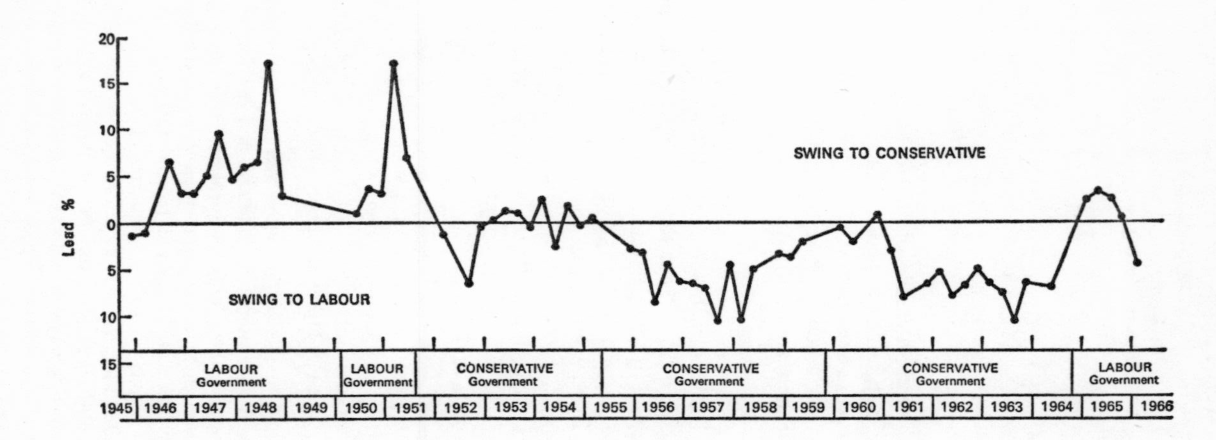

Figure 7
By-election swings 1945–66—Quarterly averages.

Table 19—Swings in by-elections and general elections

Government		Swings revealed in By-elections (average during Parliament)	Subsequent general election	Improvement for party in office
1945	Lab.	C 3·6	C 2·8	+0·8
1950	Lab.	C 4·3	C 0·9	+3·4
1951	Con.	C 0·2	C 2·1	+1·9
1955	Con.	L 4·8	C 1·1	+5·9
1959	Con.	L 5·5	L 3·1	+2·4
1964	Lab.	C 1·6	L 2·6	+4·2

In considering the significance of by-election results, therefore, whilst it is usually justifiable to assume that the trend revealed by a series of by-elections over a period of time is probably correct, it would be prudent to conclude that the government's standing is a little higher than the results indicate.

Local Elections[6]

Apart from Parliamentary by-elections, the most important subsidiary elections held in Britain are those of representatives on local authorities. Each year, in May, elections are held to fill one-third of the elective places[7] on each of the 352 borough councils, and similar elections are held for the great majority of the 538 urban and 473 rural district councils, though in a minority of these the whole council comes up for election at three-yearly intervals. In addition, the membership of the fifty-eight county councils is elected every three years, in April, and in London both the Greater London Council and the thirty-two London Borough Councils are re-elected at three-yearly intervals. Finally, the rural districts are sub-divided into parishes, most of which have their own councils which deal with very local matters. Altogether, there are about 7,500 parish councils, and these are elected every three years, in May.

[6] The details related in this section refer only to England and Wales. The structure of local government in Scotland and in Northern Ireland differs to some extent, and though the electoral system is virtually identical to England and Wales there are a number of local variations. See *The Municipal Yearbook* (London, Municipal Journal Ltd., annually).

[7] On borough and county councils one quarter of the members are non-elective, and are called aldermen. They are chosen by the councillors for a six-year term, and half retire every three years. Apart from not being able to take part in the election of other aldermen, the powers of an alderman are identical to that of a councillor. There are no aldermen on urban and rural district councils or on parish councils: all their members are elected by popular ballot.

The boroughs and urban districts are sub-divided into a number of wards, each of which elects three councillors, one of whom retires each year. The counties are divided into electoral divisions returning one member each. The arrangement of electoral areas for rural district and parish councils is determined by the county council in whose area they are included. In London the arrangements are different. It was laid down under the London Government Act of 1963, which re-organized local government in the Greater London area, that eventually the electoral areas for the Greater London Council should correspond to the Parliamentary constituencies and that each of these should elect one Greater London councillor. But it was stipulated that this provision should take effect only after the subsequent Parliamentary re-distribution, and that in the interim the London boroughs should form the electoral districts, each returning either two, three or four members, and that the voters should have, respectively, either two, three or four votes. This system applied in the first two GLC elections, in 1964 and 1967. The London boroughs are themselves divided into wards represented by varying numbers of councillors, each of whom retire simultaneously every three years, in May.

Voters who are qualified to vote in Parliamentary elections are also entitled to vote in local government elections for the councils in whose area they reside. In addition, peers are permitted to vote and, also, occupiers of any rateable land or premises in the area (this would apply mostly to businessmen and tradesmen) of a yearly value of £10 or more. No person, however, may vote more than once in an election for the same council. Peers and non-residential voters are included on the electoral register with the prefix L, indicating that they are not entitled to vote at Parliamentary elections. The numbers involved in these two extra categories are not large, and the electorate is substantially the same in both types of election.

To be a candidate in a local election it is necessary to be "of full age" (*i.e.* twenty-one), a local government elector for the area of the local authority concerned or own freehold or leasehold land in the area, or have resided there for twelve months preceding the date of the election. There are, however, a number of disqualifications—the most important being that employees of a local authority may not seek election to it. This excludes quite a number of people, for example teachers, who would otherwise be eligible. If, however, a teacher is employed by a county council it would not exclude him from seeking election to a borough or district council, even if his school were situated in its area.

As in the case of Parliamentary candidates, it is necessary to be nominated by ten electors for the ward or electoral area concerned. There is also a statutory limit to the amount of expenditure which a candidate may incur. The sum allowed is £25 for the first 500 electors and 2d. for each elector in excess of 500. Where there are two joint candidates the maximum expenditure for each is reduced by one-fourth, and if there are three or more joint candidates the maximum is reduced by one-third. Table 20 shows the limits for various sizes of electorate. Unlike Parliamentary candidates, few candidates in local elections spend anything near the limit laid down.

Table 20—Expenses in local elections

Electorate	*Maximum expenditure per candidate*		
	One candidate	*Two candidates standing jointly*	*Three or more candidates standing jointly*
	£ *s. d.*	£ *s. d.*	£ *s. d.*
500	25 0 0	18 15 0	16 13 4
1,000	29 3 4	21 17 6	19 8 11
2,000	37 10 0	28 2 6	25 0 0
5,000	62 10 0	46 17 6	41 13 4
10,000	104 3 4	78 2 6	69 8 11

The ballot papers for local elections are similar to Parliamentary ones, and, again, there is no provision for party labels. This is a greater handicap for local government electors, as the names of candidates are likely to be less well known than those in Parliamentary elections. In London borough elections, and those for the GLC, where multiple vacancies occur, it is especially difficult. In the Pembridge Ward of Kensington and Chelsea, for instance, in the May 1964 election, there were nineteen candidates for six seats, and each voter had six votes. As the candidates were listed alphabetically, it was a considerable task to remember the names of the six nominees of the voter's choice and to pick out the names on the paper. The evidence suggests that on this occasion, as on many others, numerous mistakes were made. The case for including party labels on the ballot paper is overwhelming.[8]

In most other respects the legal provisions for the conduct of

[8] However, the difficulties which might ensue from such a reform should not be underestimated. These include conflicts about who owns a party label—particularly likely to arise in the event of a party split such as occurred in the Liberal Party in 1918–22 and again after 1931. The necessity of obtaining legal judgements on this point would make party affairs justiciable, and might lead, e.g., to would-be candidates going to law about allegedly improper selection procedures. There would also be the problem of preventing independents from using official-sounding labels.

local elections are the same as for Parliamentary contests,[9] and, on a more restricted scale, the candidates run a similar type of campaign. But there are a number of important differences. At general elections between 75 and 85 per cent of the registered voters go to the polls, at local elections the figure seldom rises above 50 per cent, and the average is not more than 40 per cent. At a general election virtually all seats are contested by both Labour and Conservative candidates, while in local elections this is true only of urban areas. In the countryside there are relatively few contests on party lines, and even in the towns there is a fairly large number of unopposed returns. Moreover, local issues and the personalities of individual candidates clearly have a strong influence in local elections, though a high proportion of electors who cast their votes do so out of loyalty to their national party allegiances.

Nevertheless, the results of local elections are closely scrutinized as guides to political trends, particularly those in London, in the boroughs throughout the country and in the more industrialized counties such as Lancashire, Nottinghamshire, Staffordshire and Yorkshire (West Riding), in all of which the great majority of the seats are contested on a party political basis. On rare occasions, when a particularly outstanding change in political control is registered, it can have a substantial impact on the national political scene. In 1934, for instance, Labour won control of the former London County Council for the first time, and this gave a tremendous boost to a party which had been in the doldrums since its disastrous defeat in the 1931 general election. Similarly, the capture by the Conservatives of the GLC in April 1967 went a long way to restore Tory morale after a lengthy period without electoral success.

More generally, the total gains and losses each year in the borough elections are taken as a barometer of the parties' standing in the country, though account has to be taken of the fact that the seats contested were last fought three years previously. With this proviso, there is much evidence that these results do give an accurate reflection of public opinion, though, as in the case of by-

Similar problems have, however, been overcome in other democratic countries, and they do not, in the author's view, invalidate the case for reform. An ingenious alternative solution for overcoming the confusion in multi-member wards in local elections has been suggested to the author by Mr David Butler. He proposes that any candidates who so choose may be permitted to be bracketed together, without party labels, and that each grouping should draw lots to decide its position on the ballot paper.

[9] See A. Norman Schofield, *Local Elections* (London, Chas. Knight and Co., 1962) for the detailed provisions.

elections, there is a tendency to exaggerate the swing against the government party. As political barometers, however, local elections are unsatisfactory, as they take place only once a year. Attempts to use local government by-elections, which occur at frequent intervals but receive very little publicity, as political indicators have so far proved inconclusive.[10]

[10] See *The Economist*, March 19th and 26th, 1966.

12. Opinion Polls

APART FROM TELEVISION, THE MOST IMPORTANT NEW FACTOR WHICH has influenced elections in the post-war period has been the public opinion polls. No politician worth his salt is now ignorant of the latest state of the parties, as revealed in the columns of the *Daily Mail* or *The Daily Telegraph*; and at closely fought by-elections the predictions of the pollsters receive incomparably more attention than the pronouncements of the candidates.

This is all a very recent development. On the eve of the 1945 general election the Gallup poll reported in the *News Chronicle* a Labour lead over the Conservatives of 6 per cent. Nobody took the slightest notice of this; least of all the *News Chronicle*. So far from predicting a runaway Labour victory, the political correspondent of that paper wrote that "the final result may well prove very near a stalemate." The most popular prediction in the other papers was a Conservative majority of "around one hundred," and none of them mentioned the Gallup poll forecast. The lack of interest in the Gallup predictions in 1945 is, in itself, a commentary on British insularity, for nine years previously the methods of public opinion polls had been sensationally vindicated in an American presidential election.

The man who introduced opinion polling into Britain was Dr Henry Durant. In 1936 he set up the British Institute of Public Opinion, normally known as the Gallup Poll, under the sponsorship of the *News Chronicle*, which published its findings from 1938 to 1960. The British Gallup poll has close connections with its American namesake, and often co-operates with it and other Gallup affiliates in international surveys, but it has complete financial and managerial independence. Since 1963 it has been a wholly-owned subsidiary of S. G. Warburg's, the merchant bankers. Now in his mid-sixties, and still the head of the organization, which is now known as Social Surveys (Gallup Poll) Ltd., Dr Durant is the doyen of British opinion pollsters. His firm has carried out surveys of political opinion nearly every month since October 1938, has predicted the result of every general election since 1945 and of over forty by-elections. It employs some 1,800 part-time interviewers, and its market research activities are probably ten times as extensive as its political polling work. As well as the regular questions on voting intention, a large number of further questions of a socio-political nature are included in Gallup questionnaires, which often yield valuable evidence of changing public attitudes over the years. Since the demise of the *News Chronicle* in 1960, Gallup findings have been published in *The Daily Telegraph* and the *Sunday Telegraph*.

The *Daily Mail*'s National Opinion Polls Ltd. was founded in 1958, as a subsidiary company of Associated Newspapers. Its founder, Mr R. M. Shields, had worked for a short period with the Gallup poll and up to the 1959 election he employed Gallup staff to do his interviewing. Since then, NOP has had its own corps of interviewers, and its methods vary from those of the Gallup poll in many particulars. As newcomers in the field, NOP began to specialize in by-election predictions, which resulted in a large harvest of publicity. NOP are responsible for media research for Allied Newspapers and, like Gallup, do a great deal of commercial market research. The findings of the Gallup and NOP polls are presented in somewhat different ways. The *Daily Mail* gives rather more prominence to the NOP results which, during by-election campaigns, have often formed the main news story. But as it is a popular paper with limited space, fewer details about the questions and answers are normally given than in *The Daily Telegraph*'s reports on the Gallup poll. Both Gallup and NOP produce private subscription bulletins which give the results of their surveys in much greater detail.

Gallup and NOP are the only organizations in Britain which take continuous soundings of public opinion, but there are several others which conduct opinion polls from time to time. The longest standing is the *Daily Express* Poll of Public Opinion, which has been publishing findings intermittently since 1943 and which has attempted to forecast the result of each general election since 1950. The *Daily Express* poll does no commercial market research work and is excessively coy about its methods, which are a mystery to other people working in the same field. Research Services Ltd., a flourishing market research firm under the directorship of Dr Mark Abrams, has conducted polls during three general election campaigns—1951 (for the *Daily Sketch*) and 1964 and 1966 (for *The Observer*). They have also conducted other occasional polls, usually commissioned by American academic sources, though their most publicized survey was carried out on behalf of *Socialist Commentary*, in an attempt to explain Labour's defeat in the 1959 general election.[1] A number of other market research firms have undertaken polls in individual constituencies on behalf of newspapers (notably in the 1966 general election), while some provincial papers, and the London *Evening Standard*, have carried out their own constituency polls.

The normal national sample of both the Gallup poll and the NOP includes between 1,000 and 2,000 respondents. During election campaigns, however, larger samples are by no means infrequent—the final survey of the Gallup poll before the 1964 election, for example, included 3,829 interviews.

For the man in the street the main interest in opinion polls is in whether they can succeed in picking the winner at a general election. In this respect, the polls (with the exception of the *Daily Express* poll) have had a perfect record, as far as British general elections are concerned. Gallup, NOP and Research Services have picked the correct winner at each of the general elections which they have covered; the *Daily Express* poll has had the misfortune of picking the losing side twice (in 1950 and 1964) and of recording the widest margin of error of any poll (in 1966). The record of the various polls in the general elections since the war is shown in Table 21.

In 1951 all the polls predicted a greater total vote for the Conservatives, though in the event more people voted for Labour. But as the Conservatives won more seats in the House of Commons and were able to form a government, they could still claim to have picked the winner. The degree of accuracy of the two leading British polls (Gallup and NOP) is comparable to that of the principal polling organizations in the United States, Germany, France and other countries in forecasting the results of major elections. The *usual* margin of error is well under 2 per cent (and the maximum has been under 4 per cent). It should be fairly safe to conclude, in future British general elections, that if the polls' final forecasts show one party leading the other by more than 4 per cent it is highly probable that they will have picked the winner. Forecasts of victory by a narrower margin should command less confidence. If the polls vary markedly it is advisable to take an average between them.

The margin of error for by-elections and for individual constituencies in general elections is much larger. Between 1959 and 1965 the Gallup poll covered eleven by-elections; its average error in

[1] See Mark Abrams, Richard Rose and Rita Hinden, *Must Labour Lose?* (London, Penguin, 1960).

Table 21—General Election Forecasts

Percentage gap between major parties (Great Britain only):

		Forecast	*Error**
1945	Gallup	6·0	3·4
	Actual gap	9·4	
1950	Gallup	1·5	1·1
	Daily Express	0·5	2·1
	Actual gap	2·6	
1951	Gallup	−2·5	3·3
	Daily Express	−4·0	4·8
	Research Services	−7·0	7·8
	Actual gap	0·8	
1955	Gallup	3·5	0·2
	Daily Express	2·7	0·6
	Actual gap	3·3	
1959	Gallup	2·0	2·2
	Daily Express	3·7	0·5
	NOP	3·9	0·3
	Actual gap	4·2	
1964	Gallup	2·0	0·1
	Daily Express	−0·8	2·7
	NOP	3·1	1·2
	Research Services	1·0	0·9
	Actual gap	1·9	
1966	Gallup	11·0	3·7
	Daily Express	16·7	9·4
	NOP	9·0	1·7
	Research Services	8·1	0·8
	Actual gap	7·3	

*The margin of error shown here tends to exaggerate the inaccuracy of the polls, as the error involved in forecasting the gap between the two leading parties is usually larger than the average error in the estimate of each party's vote. Nevertheless, it has been followed throughout in this chapter, as the gap between the parties is normally the most significant feature of a poll forecast.

predicting the gap between the two leading candidates was 7·1 per cent, and it picked the wrong winner twice. In the same period NOP did twenty-two by-election polls, with an average error of 6·7 per cent and put the wrong party ahead on three occasions. At the 1966 election fifty-five individual constituencies were polled by various polling organizations, with an average error of 5·8 per cent (for details see Appendix 8 on page 175). There are good reasons why it is more difficult to get an accurate result in a single constituency than in a national sample. A scratch organization must be set up on each occasion, and there are no previous poll results for the constituency, against which to check trends. Furthermore, in a national poll errors in one area tend to be cancelled out by others, in the opposite direction, elsewhere. Above all, there is no way of accurately forecasting the turn-out at a by-election and of relating it to voting intention.

Things are made worse by the refusal of most newspapers which sponsor local polls to provide sufficient funds for a large enough sample to be interviewed. In theory, as the electorate of the average constituency is less than 60,000 a much smaller absolute sample should yield comparable results to the minimum of 1,000 which is normally regarded as essential for national surveys. In practice, it does not work out like that, and there are reasons for believing that 1,000 is the minimum necessary to get good results in individual constituencies. Many constituency surveys involve no more than 300–400 interviews, so it is not really surprising that some of the predictions have been hopelessly wrong. But even the best conducted local polls have shown margins of error much greater than in national forecasts, and in the view of the present author the utility of polls in individual constituencies is seriously open to question.

From 1945 onwards the fame and prestige of the polls steadily increased (though in 1948, as in other countries, there was a marked setback due to the United States' polls' fiasco in picking Dewey to beat Truman[2]). In 1963, however, doubts began to arise because of discrepancies between the findings of the two principal polls, Gallup and NOP. On several occasions in 1963 and 1964 the two polls differed by as much as 10 per cent in the size of the Labour lead which they reported, though the polls converged in their final predictions before the 1964 election. Since that period the polls have often diverged considerably in their findings, but usually by a more narrow margin. To some extent, the reasons for the disparity between the polls are still a puzzle, but for the most part they can be explained by the facts that the polls are seldom strictly comparable because their fieldwork is not usually done during exactly the same period and that the polls use different sampling methods. At this point, it should, perhaps, be stressed that the size of the sample is less important than its representative nature. A badly drawn sample of two million can be much less accurate than a well constructed one of a thousand or so, as was demonstrated in the 1936 presidential election in the United States, when the *Literary Digest* poll,

[2] The main reason for their error was that they stopped polling two whole weeks before polling day, and failed to detect a late ground-swell to Truman. This is one error they are unlikely to repeat. See Mosteller, Frederick, *et al.*, *The Pre-election Polls of 1948* (New York, Social Service Research Council, 1949).

with 2,376,533 respondents predicted a landslide victory for the Republican candidate, while Gallup accurately forecast an easy win for Roosevelt.

There are two principal methods of constructing a polling sample. The NOP uses a *random* sample—taking every hundredth or thousandth name from the election register and calling on the voters in their own homes. Gallup normally uses a *quota* sample, instructing its interviewers to contact so many voters of each sex, age group, occupation and social class, worked out in proportion to the total population. Neither method provides a perfect sample, but they have different shortcomings. Under the quota method, by which people are interviewed in the street, it is the elderly infirm who are left out. In a random sample, in which people are interviewed in their own homes, young people who tend to spend most of their time out are invariably under-represented. The random sample, which involves contacting named individuals and calling back several times if they are out, is much more expensive than the quota system. The consensus of opinion is, however, that it is more reliable, and Gallup now uses a random as well as a quota sample for its final pre-election predictions.

Occasional marked variations between the polls should not cause concern; indeed, it would be more suspicious if they were always in agreement. When there are consistent differences it is probably safer to be guided by the *average* of the two polls rather than to depend exclusively on either one of them. Both the polls could effect improvements in their methods which should ensure a higher degree of accuracy. Such improvements (notably the employment of full-time trained interviewers in place of untrained part-timers) would be expensive, and it is unrealistic to criticize the polls for failing to implement them. The blame should rather attach to their clients, *The Daily Telegraph* and the *Daily Mail*, who seem to be quite happy to receive poll findings on the cheap (their joint annual expenditure is probably less than £100,000) rather than to pay extra for more reliable results. This cheese-paring attitude is less in evidence in the *Daily Mail*, which did at least agree to the NOP going over to random sampling when it was represented that this would be more accurate. But neither newspaper appears to have much understanding of the significance of the polls whose results they publish, nor to show much concern about their mechanics. This is unfortunate, as nobody else is in a position to take a continuous interest in their affairs and to provide a check on their activities. Much the greatest stimulus to the polls to improve their methods is the fact that there are *two* of them (apart from those which carry out occasional surveys). Competition keeps both polls on their toes; this is one field where monopoly could be very dangerous.

Some critics of opinion polls have suggested that they may create a bandwagon effect in favour of the party which they report to be in the lead. There have even been demands, on these grounds, for polls to be made illegal, by, among others, two Tory MPs, Aidan Crawley in 1962 and Gresham Cooke in 1966, demands which were repudiated on the latter occasion by both Harold Wilson and Edward Heath. The pollsters deny vehemently that there is a bandwagon effect, and indeed any careful examination of the evidence should make it clear that, at least in Britain, any such effect is of minimal proportions.[3]

Although polls do not appear to affect the way in which people vote, to any great extent, they clearly influence the morale of party activists, though even here the effect it has on their efforts cannot easily be predicted. A disappointing poll may lead to a slackening of effort or to gestures of defiance which give a sharper edge to a party's campaign—a favourable one may equally lead to complacency or renewed dedication. More importantly, polls have a very considerable influence on the behaviour of politicians. The importance of polls in informing the Prime Minister of favourable occasions for holding a general election, and even more importantly, warning him off unfavourable ones, has already been stressed in an earlier chapter. But the whole tenor of the last three election campaigns has been dominated by opinion poll findings—especially that of 1966 when the knowledge that Labour was a long way ahead was the seminal fact of the campaign.

Although the opinion polls have established such an important role for themselves in British politics, in one respect they have played a much smaller part in Britain than in the United States and some other countries. This is in the use of privately commissioned polls by the parties and by individual political leaders. Largely because of the absence of primary elections, the commissioning of polls by politicians is unknown in Britain, and is likely to remain so. Even the parties themselves have been cautious in their use of opinion polling, and they have used it mainly to test

[3] See articles in *Encounter*, by H. J. Eysenck (Feb., 1965) suggesting the existence of a bandwagon effect, and replies by Henry Durant (March, 1965) and the present author (August, 1965). Other useful comments were made by G. P. Hyett (April, 1965), Angus Campbell (May, 1965) and Seymour Martin Lipset (July, 1965). Professor Eysenck replied to the comments in the October, 1965, issue.

propaganda themes and for copy-testing of posters, newspaper advertisements and other visual material.

The first campaign to be based, to any significant degree, on material gleaned from the polls was that launched by the Conservatives before the 1959 election.[4] Labour was slower off the mark, but relied to a similar extent on privately commissioned polls for its run-up campaign to the 1964 election.[5] Since 1964 the Conservatives have retained the services of a new public opinion organization (the Opinion Research Centre), which has worked almost exclusively for them. The Liberals, too, from time to time, have made limited use of privately commissioned polls.

This comparatively recent development has been unfavourably received in some quarters, and allegations have been made that politicians have subordinated their principles to the desire to win votes.[6] People holding this view appear to be ignorant of the manner in which politicians make decisions. Opinion polls are only one of a large number of factors which they have to take into account, and it is clear that they usually come a long way down the list. Indeed, it has been argued forcefully and effectively by Richard Rose that politicians lack the necessary knowledge and interest to evaluate the poll material to which they do have access, and that its influence on them is quite disproportionately small.[7]

It is, in fact, a totally unrealistic view that polls can tell a politician what policies he ought to adopt. Any political leader who allowed them to do so would soon develop a reputation for irresolution and lack of consistency. The most that a poll can do for a politician or a party is to help them to put over, in an effective way, the policies on which they have already decided. It is difficult to see anything improper or dishonourable in this.

[4] See *Public Opinion Polls and Political Parties* by Mark Abrams, paper read to the American Sociological Association, September, 1962, and Lord Windlesham, *Communication and Political Power*, *op. cit.*, pp. 35–62.

[5] See Richard Rose, *Influencing Voters*, *op. cit.*, pp. 60–87.

[6] See, for example, the article by Alan Watkins, "Rationality, Reason and Dr. Rose," *The Spectator*, 13 January, 1967.

[7] See Richard Rose, *op. cit.*, pp. 219–26.

13. How People Vote

THE BRITISH VOTER IS SUBJECTED TO A HEAVY BARRAGE OF PROPAganda from all three major parties, and to occasional salvoes from minor groups and independents, during election campaigns and, to a lesser degree, at other times. Earlier chapters of this book have sought to describe the various ways in which the parties seek to influence public opinion. This chapter will attempt to discern whether all this activity makes much difference to the way that people vote.

The short answer is "not much." The first impression which British elections make on the observer is one of overwhelming solidity in the support of each party.

Table 22—Parents' influence on voting

Respondent's party choice	*Father's pre-war voting behaviour* Con.	*Lab.*	*Lib.*	*Not known*	*Never voted*
Con.	71	28	36	48	44
Lab.	15	61	24	31	44
Other*	14	11	40	21	12

*Includes Liberals, don't knows and would abstain.

The majority of voters form their voting habits during their youth and do not deviate thereafter. Moreover, hereditary influences appear to be extremely strong, as several studies have shown that most electors vote the same way as their parents. A poll undertaken by Dr Mark Abrams in 1960, for instance, showed that 71 per cent of the children of Conservative fathers and 61 per cent of those of Labour fathers were voting for the same party. See Table 22.[1] The allegiance of a large, but decreasing proportion of voters is determined predominantly by social class. It is known that in every post-war election a large majority of middle-class voters have supported the Conservative Party and that over half of the manual workers have voted Labour.

[1] Taken from Mark Abrams, "Social Trends and Electoral Behaviour," *British Journal of Sociology*, XIII: 3 (1962).

Table 23—Voting intention by social class, 1966
(Gallup poll figures)

	Upper (5%)	*Middle* (22%)	*Working* (62%)	*Very poor* (11%)
Con.	78	63	30	21
Lab.	8	22	57	65
Lib.	9	8	6	6
Other	0	0	1	1
Don't Know	5	7	7	9

The voting intention figures for the different social classes, as revealed in the final Gallup poll before the 1966 general election, are shown in Table 23. In this election Labour did better than at any previous contest since 1945, and its figures in the two highest social groups are about double what they had been in 1959. At most post-war general elections only about 10 per cent of the middle class voters have supported Labour. On the other hand, the Conservative Party has always appeared to enjoy the support of a substantial minority of working class voters, seldom falling much below one-third. This has led a recent writer to comment on what he calls "this strange paradox": "The middle class claims not to believe in classes, yet its vote seems to uphold the classical Marxian division of society into two main classes. The manual working class is said to be class-conscious and it has at its disposal a party which caters mainly for the working class, but not more than two-thirds of its votes goes to that party."[2]

Among members of trade unions, however, support for Labour is much more solid—surveys have consistently shown that trade unionists are three or four times more likely to vote Labour than Conservative. Manual workers who are not members of trade unions show much less resistance to the notion of voting Conservative, and the Labour lead amongst them is much narrower. Moreover, it was shown in one study[3] that workers in small family firms are more likely to vote Conservative than those in larger "non-traditional" firms. There is also continuing overwhelming evidence that workers in the older heavier industries—such as coal mining, shipbuilding and steel—are much more solidly Labour than the remainder of the manual working class.[4]

[2] J. Blondel, *Voters, Parties and Leaders* (London, Penguin, 1963), p. 58.

[3] Margaret Stacey, *Tradition and Change: A Study of Banbury* (Oxford University Press, 1960), p. 46.

[4] See, *inter alia*, A. J. Allen, *The English Voter* (London, English Universities Press, 1964), pp. 108–22.

With rising standards of living and a gradual blurring of class divisions, non-class factors are beginning to determine the electoral choice of an increasing number of voters. Moreover, the continuing efforts which the Labour Party has made, particularly since Harold Wilson became its leader, to shed its cloth-cap image appear to have enjoyed a wide measure of success, and it was notable in both the 1964 and 1966 elections that Labour made relatively greater advances in middle class areas than elsewhere, though this was not uniformly true of all parts of the country.[5] But it seems likely that for many years to come social class will remain the largest single factor influencing voters.

The next most important is almost certainly that of sex. Studies in many democratic countries have shown that women are more to the right than men, and in no country is the evidence for this stronger than in Britain. In fact, the Gallup poll has shown that a majority of men voters have supported Labour at every general election since 1945, whereas women voters have shown a majority for the Conservatives six times out of seven. (See Table 24.) As women voters outnumber men, the Labour lead among male voters has to be greater than the Conservative lead among women for a Labour government to be returned.

Table 24—Voting Intention by Sex

General election	1945	1950	1951	1955	1959	1964	1966
	%	%	%	%	%	%	%
Men							
Con.	36½	41	47	46½	45½	40	36½
Lab.	55	47	50	51	47½	49½	56
Lib.	8½	12	3	2½	7	10½	7½
Lab. lead	18½	6	3	4½	2	9½	19½
Women							
Con.	43½	44½	50	55	51	45½	46
Lab.	46½	43½	46	42½	43	39½	45
Lib.	10	12	4	2½	6	15	9
Lab. lead	3	—	—	—	—	—	—
Con. lead	—	1	4	12½	8	6	1

Source: The Gallup poll. Figures show only supporters of three main parties. Quota sample used throughout.

The reasons for the conservatism of women voters have been much discussed, and the most favoured explanations are that, psychologically, they tend to be more cautious, and that this innate

[5] See Butler and King (1964), *op. cit.*, pp. 338–42; and Butler and King (1966), *op. cit.*, pp. 265–77.

tendency is reinforced by their preoccupation with domestic concerns (Bismarck's *Kinder, Kirche, Küche*.) It might be added that their lack of trade union membership (in 1966 only 1,747,000 women belonged to TUC unions compared with 7,120,000 men) insulates them from the most powerful institutional influence in favour of voting Labour. Whatever the reason, it is clear that for the last two to three decades the Conservative Party has managed to keep on fairly even terms with Labour only because of its appeal to women voters.

The most perceptive analysis of the electorate yet to appear was made by Dr Mark Abrams in 1964.[6] He wrote then "each party can rely upon the unwavering support of approximately one-third of the electorate. Their devotion is unaffected by any shortcomings in party leadership, party programme, constituency, candidate or party organization.... The remaining uncommitted one-third of the electorate do not form a homogeneous group. Its members are drawn from both sexes, all social statuses, and all age groups... no more than half of them will usually vote."

This final third of the electorate (sometimes referred to as the floating vote) is made up of a number of overlapping sub-groups. These are Liberal voters, abstainers, lukewarm supporters of either party and genuine floaters. Liberal voters are a much more heterogeneous collection than their Labour or Conservative counterparts. A large proportion of both Labour and Conservative voters are regular supporters of their party. It is doubtful if more than a third of the electors who vote for Liberal candidates regard themselves as Liberals. The remainder are mostly disgruntled supporters of the larger parties or those who vote Liberal at a particular election because of the personal qualities of the candidate. Although the level of Liberal support in the opinion polls does not vary greatly—for some years it has fluctuated around 10 per cent (except in the aftermath of the Orpington by-election when it was much higher)—it is very probable that the actual composition of this 10 per cent fluctuates greatly.

Abstainers are, again, a very mixed group. Some are persistent abstainers, and some only temporary. There are, first, what might be termed "involuntary" abstainers—those who have been accidentally left off the register, or who have moved and inadvertently failed to claim a postal vote, or who are ill or who for some other pressing reason genuinely find it difficult to get along to the polling station on election day. At a rough estimate, these might add up to

[6] See "Opinion Polls and Party Propaganda," *Public Opinion Quarterly*, Vol. 28, Spring 1964, pp. 13–19.

about 10 per cent of the electorate, which leaves an equal number of "voluntary" abstainers—people who could easily cast their votes but who choose not to do so.

Probably a small proportion of these are discriminating electors who choose not to vote because they do not approve of the candidates or parties which are running in their constituencies. For example, it seems likely that in 1964 one-fifth, and in 1966 one-quarter, of would-be Liberal voters in constituencies without Liberal candidates stayed at home rather than give their votes to non-Liberals.[7] But the majority of abstainers are among the least discriminating of electors—those who have the least interest in and the smallest knowledge of current political issues. They tend to be concentrated amongst the poorest and least educated sections of the population, the very old, the very young and more among women than among men. Successive polls have shown that among non-voters a higher proportion are sympathetic to Labour than to the Conservatives, and it is generally considered that a high turn-out favours Labour, while a low one is to the advantage of the Tories.

Finally, and most elusive, are the people who actually switch their votes from one major party to the other. It is extremely difficult to locate this category, but a study of a single constituency—Bristol North-East in 1955[8]—does give us a rough idea of their total number. The authors discovered that 6 per cent of the Conservative voters of 1955 were Labour voters in 1951, and that 6 per cent of Labour voters in 1955 were Conservative voters in 1951. In the absence of any more detailed studies (and opinion poll evidence has so far proved inconclusive) this finding must be treated with some caution, but a figure of 6 per cent of major party voters switching at an average general election does not sound implausible, though normally one would not expect the changes to cancel out exactly, as they appear to have done on this occasion.

But, despite the increasing interest which sociologists have, since 1945, shown in elections and in voting habits, little is known about what actually causes people to change their voting allegiances. There is evidence[9] that many more people switch over between elections rather than during election campaigns. This has led the parties to begin their active campaigning at a much earlier stage than in the past. Hence the Conservatives' highly successful poster campaign (on the theme of "Life is better with the Conservatives—

[7] See Butler and King (1966), *op. cit.*, p. 275.

[8] See R. S. Milne and H. C. Mackenzie, *Straight Fight* (London, Hansard Society, 1958). Quoted by Blondel, *op. cit.*, p. 71.

[9] See Trenaman and McQuail, *op. cit.*

don't let Labour ruin it") in 1958–59 and the extensive Press advertising which both the major parties began in May 1963 in preparation for the general election of 1964. In the period after the 1964 election it was by no means certain, because of the government's tiny majority, when the next election would take place. Furthermore, the Conservatives, the really big spenders, were now in opposition and were unable to dictate the date of the election, and were consequently not in a position to prepare a carefully phased build-up to their campaign. In the event, neither party embarked on major pre-electoral expenditure for this election, but it may be expected that the pattern set in 1959 and 1964 will be repeated at subsequent elections.

But the majority of voters seem to be immune to direct influence by the political parties. The different items in a party's programme and the promises which it makes seem to make little difference to people's voting intentions. A glance at the charts produced by the Gallup Poll showing the fluctuations in the level of support of the different parties in the period since 1945 shows less correlation than one might expect with major political events and with the triumphs and disasters of ministers and opposition leaders. (See Figure 8, on page 145.) A closer examination reveals a high correlation with the general level of economic activity in the country. In a period of expansion, the government, whatever its political complexion, tends to prosper—a rise in the bank rate, a damper on wage claims, a restriction of credit facilities, a rise in unemployment, and its support almost invariably slumps.

Much more than the actual policies on which political parties fight elections, the voters are aware of general images, whose roots may go back far into the past. Thus the Labour Party will be seen by its supporters as the party which is opposed to privilege, which is for the welfare state, which cares for ordinary people, and by its opponents as the party of nationalization and controls, of extravagant financial policies and as the party which is *only* for the workers. The Conservative Party is seen by its supporters as the party for people who want to get on, for business efficiency and for making Britain's voice heard in the world. Its opponents see it as the party of the rich, the privileged and the old-fashioned. Nevertheless, the great majority of voters, though they remain committed to one party or the other, are willing to admit that their opponents have many virtues. Extreme partisanship is rare.[10]

Support for the parties seems sometimes to be governed more by

[10] See Mark Abrams, *Public Opinion Quarterly*, Vol. 28, Spring 1964, *op. cit.*

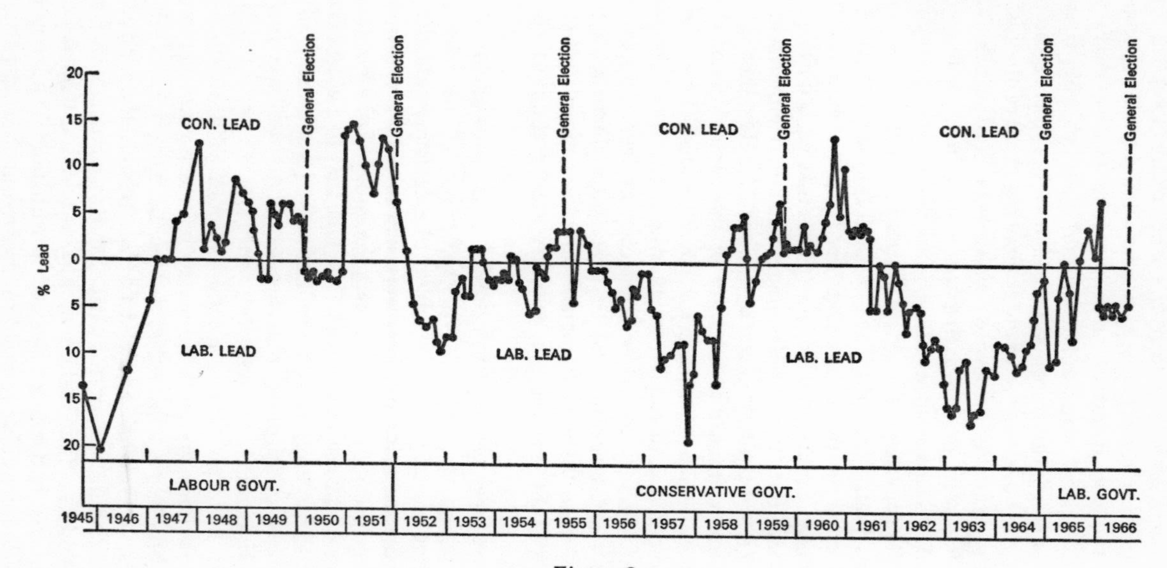

Figure 8
Party leads 1945–66—Gallup poll figures.

the activities of their natural allies than by what they do themselves. If businessmen are seen to be behaving in an abnormally rapacious manner, or a takeover battle is fought with obvious disregard to the public interest, it is the Conservative Party which suffers. Similarly, if trade unions appear to be behaving irresponsibly and, especially if strikes occur which inconvenience the public without at the same time strongly convincing them of the justice of the strikers' case, the Labour Party takes a hard knock. This is rough justice, perhaps, but each party gains considerably in financial and other ways from its alliances so they hardly complain too loudly at the compensating disadvantages.

The very small effect which the national campaigns of the parties appear to have on the voters does not by any means prove that they have been misdirected. It is probable that each party's efforts largely cancel out those of its opponents, but if either were unilaterally to desist it would mean a walk-over for the other side. And it is the very volume and intensity of the campaigns of the two larger parties which guarantee for them a monopoly of the votes of some 90 per cent of the electorate. Any reduction of their efforts would open the way to one or other of them being supplanted by the Liberals or some other smaller party. Most knowledgeable observers now take the view that the main object of an election campaign is to rally wavering supporters rather than to convince opponents.

In one respect, television has proved a far more effective means of campaigning than any previously known. It has been established[11] that in 1959, as a result of the television election programmes, the majority of voters were substantially better informed than in any previous election about the issues of the election and the policies of the various parties. The fact that few voters actually changed their intentions as a result of these programmes, in 1959, does not necessarily mean that this would be the case in future elections. It is much too soon fully to gauge the effect that television will have on British elections, but it is likely to be far-reaching. Perhaps the most important influence that television has had is in building up the reputation of the party leaders—Harold Macmillan, Jo Grimond and Harold Wilson being the most notable examples. The failure of Sir Alec Douglas-Home to master the medium, and the relative lack of success which attended Edward Heath's efforts, had a great deal to do with the ascendancy which Harold Wilson was able to build up in the mid-1960's.

If the national campaigns of the parties appear to have had little

[11] See particularly, Trenaman and McQuail, *op. cit.*, Chapter X.

effect on people's voting, what of the campaigns in the constituencies? In the period before the First World War many voters were probably directly influenced by these campaigns. But, as we have seen, the growth of the mass media has shifted attention overwhelmingly away from the individual candidates towards the party leaders. The result has been that neither the personality of the candidate nor the quality of his campaign has much effect on the average voter.

Nearly all authorities agree that virtually no candidate, however outstanding, is worth more than 500 extra votes to his party, and the great majority of candidates are clearly worth much less. This is not true of by-elections, where voters are relieved of the responsibility of helping to choose a government and more of them feel freer to give weight to personality factors. It is also less true of Liberal candidates than of those representing the two larger parties. But it remains true that in the great majority of constituencies, the most distinguished of statesmen can hope to win very few extra votes than would the most mediocre of party hacks. If there are constituencies where the personality of the candidate and even more important, the trouble which he is prepared to take to serve his constituents, are still significant factors they are those in the most remote parts of Scotland and Wales. But there are probably less than a dozen of these remaining.

Nor does the efficiency of the party machine in the constituencies appear to have much influence on the result. Every party worker is vividly aware of specific voters who were got to the poll *only* because of his powers of persuasion or because he gave them a lift to the poll at the last possible hour. But the sum total of these achievements does not amount to a great deal. The number of people voting in constituencies in which each party has a high level of organization is only fractionally higher than the turn-out in those constituencies where party organization is most rudimentary.[12]

One field in which organization does make a measurable contribution is postal voting. There is no doubt that the Conservatives have been much more successful in registering postal voters than their opponents. As around 2 per cent or more of votes cast in recent general elections have been postal votes, it is clear that, in closely contested constituencies postal voters can spell the difference between victory and defeat. It seems highly probable that the Conservatives have gained between five and fifteen extra seats at each election since 1950 because of their greater success in this sphere. This may be a small number, but in 1950, when Labour was re-

[12] See Butler and Rose, *op. cit.*, pp. 194–5.

turned by a majority of seven and, according to H. G. Nicholas, "It seems hard not to believe that the Conservatives owe at least ten seats to the postal vote,"[13] it was enough to make the difference between a small but viable majority and one which placed enormous strains on Labour MPs and led to a dissolution within two years. A similar handicap, though with less disastrous consequences, was suffered by the Labour Government of 1964.

In 1966 there were twenty-four seats in which the Conservative majority was less than the total number of postal votes (see Appendix 4). It seems probable that in about half of these this factor alone accounted for their victory.

It is probably inevitable that the Conservatives should gain some advantage from the postal vote. Middle-class voters generally are more aware of their civic rights and more ready to claim them than are manual workers and their families. But the decisive edge which the Conservatives have achieved, which ensures them more than 75 per cent of the postal votes in most constituencies, is a direct result of their more professional organization. It is here that their ability to employ more than twice as many agents as the Labour Party, and to provide them more often with clerical assistance has paid dividends. Although Labour certainly now shows more awareness of the importance of the postal vote than it did in 1950, it has only very partially succeeded in closing the gap. It is probably true that a big majority of Labour voters who move house or are taken seriously ill in the months preceding a general election do not record their votes. The number of lost Conservative votes is substantially less.

A striking fact about the British electorate is its homogeneity. There are virtually no important regional issues in British politics, except in Scotland, Wales and Northern Ireland, and in the first two of these they have remarkably little effect upon the voting. Of course, there are variations in the strengths of the parties in different parts of the country—Labour is strongest in Scotland, Wales and the north of England, whereas the Conservatives are much stronger in southern England. These variations are, however, mostly the result of social differences—a much higher proportion of the middle class, for example, lives in the south. It is remarkable that in nearly every general election the swing of opinion is almost uniform throughout the country and operating in the same direction. There have been two recent exceptions—in 1959 there were pro-Labour swings in south Lancashire and Scotland, whereas in

[13] H. G. Nicholas, *The British General Election of 1950* (London, Macmillan, 1951), p. 9.

the rest of the country the swing was to the Conservatives. This could be accounted for by regional pockets of unemployment, and it was the first time in over thirty years that there had been region-wide variations from the national trend. In 1964 two areas—the west Midlands and East Anglia showed deviant swings, but in 1966 the leftward movement was almost uniform throughout the whole country.

The degree of homogeneity is sufficient for highly accurate deductions to be made as to the composition of the House of Commons from any given percentage swing of opinion from one party to another. On the basis of recent general elections, it can be assumed, provided there is no large variation in the proportion of the vote going to the Liberals and other smaller parties, that each swing of 1 per cent between the Labour and Conservative parties will lead to between fifteen and eighteen seats changing hands. Table 25 shows the probable division of seats in the House of Commons given any likely swing in the election following that of 1966, though the figures will not be valid if a redistribution of Parliamentary seats takes place in the interim.

Table 25—Relationship between seats and votes after 1966 election

Swing to Conservative				*Swing to Labour*		
Con.	*Lab.*	*Con. lead over Lab.*		*Lab.*	*Con.*	*Lab. lead over Con.*
253	364	−111	Actual result	364	253	111
272	345	−77	1%	386	231	155
279	337	−58	2%	405	211	194
297	319	−22	3%	422	194	228
316	304	12	4%	450	165	285
337	284	53	5%	471	144	327
381	242	139	7½%	511	105	406
426	196	230	10%	539	75	464

In this table allowance is made for seats that would be lost or gained by the Liberal Party as a consequence of uniform swings between the two main parties; hence the total of seats won by the two parties varies slightly. The Speaker's seat is included with Labour. (Reprinted from Michael Steed's statistical analysis in *The British General Election of 1966*, *op. cit.*)

Is it possible to forecast what the swing will be? Newspapers and party organizations have never been shy of attempting to do so, but their predictions have often proved wide of the mark. There are, however, three rather more objective yardsticks which can be applied—by-elections, local elections and public opinion polls.

Parliamentary by-elections have been used as a rough and ready measure of the Government's standing for well over a hundred years. They are still regarded as important political indicators. To read too much into them may, however, have unfortunate consequences, for, as shown in a previous chapter, there are many reasons why the result of any particular by-election may be widely misleading as a reflection of the national strength of the parties.

The trend revealed by a succession of by-elections does appear, however, from past experience to offer a fairly reliable guide to the movement of political opinion. But there is a marked tendency to exaggerate the trend against the existing government. Governments invariably do a little better in general elections than preceding by-elections would have led one to expect. The greatest drawback about by-elections as political indicators, however, is that they take place only spasmodically and a by-election held in May often proves a poor guide to political feeling in November.

This is even more true of the second of our three yardsticks—local elections. These take place only once a year—in May—except every third year when county council elections are also held in April. Local elections—particularly those for borough councils—are a remarkably accurate political barometer at the time they are held, notwithstanding the considerably lower turn-out of voters at local as compared with general elections. A further disadvantage is that rather elaborate calculations have to be made before the results of local elections, which are held on the basis of different electoral areas, can be applied to general election trends.

None of these objections apply to opinion polls which are the newest and much the most reliable of election indicators.

Opinion polls are far from perfect, but they do give much the most accurate guide to the movement of political opinion and their forecasts immediately before a general election can be relied upon, with reasonable confidence, to pick the winner, unless the gap between the two leading parties is an extremely narrow one.

14. How Much Does it Cost?

THE COST OF ELECTIONS IS LESS IN THE UNITED KINGDOM THAN IN some other democratic countries, and in particular, substantially less than in the United States. But total election expenses do amount to a considerable sum, both those chargeable to the Exchequer and to local authorities and those for which the candidates and the political parties are responsible. (This chapter deals solely with the cost of general elections; statistics are not readily available of expenses incurred in local elections, though the sums involved are undoubtedly lower. Expenditure on Parliamentary by-elections is similar to that in individual constituencies at a general election.)

There are three categories of expenditure chargeable to public funds—the cost of printing and compiling the register, the returning officers' expenses and the cost of the free postal delivery of electoral communications and of the postal vote.

Under the 1948 Representation of the People Act provision was made for the compilation of two election registers each year. In 1949 as an economy cut the number was reduced to one, thereby effecting a saving of about £650,000 per year. At present prices it would probably cost about £2 million to reintroduce a second register and thus ensure that it was kept more up-to-date.

The cost of the election register is borne equally by the Treasury and the local authorities. It is of course an annual charge and the cost in 1961–62 was £2,360,000.[1] As the register is used annually for borough council and other local government elections and every three years for county council elections, it would be unrealistic to count the whole cost of maintaining the register as part of the expense of a general election.

Other costs charged to the public, through the Treasury's Consolidated Fund, are the returning officers' expenses. These include the cost of publishing the notice of the election, and receiving and publicizing the nominations and of sending out poll cards to all electors. Much the largest expense, however, is the employing of polling-station clerks on election day and of people to count the votes after the poll has closed.

[1] In 1967 the Home Office estimated the cost at over £2½ million.

The total amount of returning officers' expenses in recent general elections is shown in Table 26.

Table 26—Returning Officers' Expenses

1945	£677,999	1955	£1,106,631
1950	£806,974	1959	£1,303,694
1951	£1,015,357	1964	£1,540,000

The total for 1966 is not yet available, but the 1964 figure worked out as an average of £2,444 per constituency. It is certainly an underestimate of the expense involved, as no adequate provision is made for the temporary diversion from other work during elections of full-time local government employees.

The Treasury derive one small but regular source of income from elections—the forfeiture of deposits. This has brought in the following sums in post-war general elections:

Table 27—Lost Deposits

Year	*Number of lost deposits*	*Total sum*
1945	163	£24,450
1950	461	£69,150
1951	96	£14,400
1955	100	£15,000
1959	116	£17,400
1964	186	£28,050
1966	237	£35,550

No estimates were published before 1964 of the cost to the Post Office of the free delivery of election literature. Since then the Post Office has been able to reclaim the amount from the Treasury. Its bill for 1964 was £605,000 and for 1966, £667,300. The postal vote cost £320,000 in 1964.

When every allowance is made for indirect expenses it seems improbable that a general election costs the public purse more than about £3,000,000 plus a proportion of the *annual* cost of maintaining the election register.

The cost to candidates and their parties of fighting elections is probably greater than the cost to the public. The amount of money which may be spent on behalf of a candidate during the actual election campaign is strictly limited by law. The campaign is usually regarded as dating from the announcement of a dissolution in the case of a general election or the date that the vacancy occurs in the case of a by-election, though the law is woolly on this point. It may be that only the shorter period following the actual dissolution (or issue of a writ) is in fact covered by the law. On the other hand, the campaign might be held to date from the announcement of a candidature and this is why all parties are careful to describe their standard bearers as *prospective* candidates until the announcement of the dissolution. The point has never been contested in the courts and, in practice, all candidates play safe and return their expenses for the longer period.

Until 1918 the whole of the returning officers' expenses in each constituency was chargeable to the candidates, and this constituted a considerable extra burden, especially for poorer candidates and parties. Since 1883 there has been a restriction on the amount which can be spent on behalf of each candidate, and though the electorate has greatly increased and the value of money depreciated, the level of permitted expenditure has been lowered both in 1918 and in 1948. The effect of this has been that the actual money expended was lower in the 1966 general election than in 1906.

Since 1948 the maximum expenditure permitted in Great Britain has been:

In county constituencies: £450 plus 2d. per elector.
In borough constituencies: £450 plus 1½d. per elector.

In Northern Ireland the limits are 2d. per elector plus an allowance for agents' fee not exceeding £75 in a county election of £50 in a borough election. This amounts in practice to about two-thirds of the allowance in Great Britain.

Candidates' personal expenses, not exceeding £100, are excluded from the limitation. The effect of this restriction is that in the average constituency the maximum expenditure permitted is about £900 per candidate.[2] The average maximum for county constituencies is about £950 and that for boroughs about £850, but as the former often contain widely scattered areas of population difficult to organize, the differential can easily be justified.

Within thirty-five days after the declaration of the result the agent of each candidate has to submit to the returning officer a complete statement of expenses incurred, together with the relevant bills and receipts. Within the following ten days the returning officer is required to publish in at least two local newspapers a summary (under seven heads) of the expenses of all candidates concerned. Within a year of the election a summary of all the accounts, together with other relevant information, is published as a Parliamentary Paper, under the title, *Return of Election Expenses.*

[2] The Speaker's Conference on Electoral Law recommended in December 1965 an increase of £300 per constituency. See page 159, below.

The amounts expended by all candidates and by those of the three main parties in general elections since 1945 were as follows:

*Table 28—Expenditure by Parliamentary Candidates**

Year	*Candidates*	*Total expenditure*	*Average per candidate*	*Con.*	*Lab.*	*Lib.*
		£	£	£	£	£
1945	1,468	1,073,216	645	780	593	532
1950	1,868	1,170,114	628	777	694	459
1951	1,376	946,013	688	773	658	488
1955	1,409	904,677	642	735	611	423
1959	1,536	1,051,217	684	761	705	532
1964	1,757	1,229,203	699	790	751	579
1966	1,707	1,136,882	667	766	726	501

* The figures in the last three columns of this table are taken from the various Nuffield election studies listed on p. 177 below.

In 1966 Conservative candidates spent on average 89 per cent of the permitted maximum, Labour candidates 84 per cent and Liberals 56 per cent. Minor party and independent candidates spent on average 41 per cent. The average for all candidates was 77 per cent.

Table 29 shows the returns made by the four candidates in a London borough constituency, Hampstead, in 1966, where the maximum permitted expenditure (excluding personal expenses) was £874.

Table 29—Election Expenses in Hampstead, 1966

Nature of expenditure	*B. C. G. Whitaker (Lab.)*	*Henry Brooke (Con.)*	*Mrs. R. R. Soskin (Lib.)*	*H. G. Baldwin (Ind.)*
	£	£	£	£
Agents	25	50	45	40
Clerks, etc.	—	9	—	—
Printing, stationery, etc.	548	670	636	297
Public meetings	28	66	30	7
Committee rooms	32	25	—	16
Miscellaneous matters	218	39	71	9
Net total	851	859	782	369
Personal expenses	43	—	—	—
Grand total	894	859	782	369

All parties consistently spend more money in respect of their successful candidates than on behalf of their unsuccessful nominees, but it is in the highly marginal seats that candidates of all parties tend to spend very near the maximum permitted. Evasion of the law is apparently now fairly widespread in marginal constituencies, according to David Butler who wrote after the 1959 election:

Agents quite often admitted to subterfuges, some plainly legal, some more dubious, by which they kept their official expenses down. Sympathetic printers could undercharge, knowing that no objection would be raised to a compensating overcharge outside election time. Equipment needed solely for the campaign could be bought in advance and then hired to the agent at a very low notional figure. Although the likelihood of either side scrutinizing its rivals' accounts or launching a petition is very small, it is unfortunate that the law should be so much circumvented.[3]

Restriction of expenditure is highly desirable if money is not to talk at election time, but in view of the virtual halving of money since the end of the last war some upward revision of the permitted limits is probably now overdue. A far more serious problem, however, is the lack of any limitation on amounts which can be spent nationally and in the period between elections.

These amounts have now begun to dwarf the total sums spent on behalf of all candidates. In the period leading up to the 1959 election it has been estimated that the Conservative Party spent £468,000 on advertising alone, while over three times this amount (£1,435,000) was spent by business firms supporting the Conservative cause. The Labour Party spent a mere £103,000 on propaganda at this time.[4]

The period leading up to the 1964 general election saw a great increase in expenditure on political advertising. The Conservatives spent just under one million pounds (£992,000) and private business interests (mainly steel firms) nearly two million (£1,896,000). For the first time the Labour Party attempted to match the expenditure of its opponents; it spent £314,000—a small sum in comparison, but unprecedentedly large for a party which has made a practice of parading its poverty.[5] Neither the Liberals nor any of the minor parties were able to make a comparable effort.

National expenditure on this scale goes a long way to thwart the intention of Parliament in restricting the level of expenditure in the constituencies. This has led to a growing demand for an enquiry into the whole subject of election expenditure, and when the Speaker's Conference on Electoral Law was appointed in May 1965 this was one of the subjects which it was invited to examine.[6]

[3] Butler and Rose, *op. cit.*, pp. 144–5.

[4] For detailed estimates see Butler and Rose, *op. cit.*, pp. 21, 28, 252.

[5] Figures estimated by Richard Rose in *The British General Election of 1964, op. cit.*, pp. 369–80. See also *Influencing Voters, op. cit.*

[6] See Chapter 15, below. The Conference declined to recommend any restriction on expenditure between elections.

15. An Evolving System

IN 1254 THE SHERIFF OF EACH COUNTY WAS ORDERED TO SEND TWO knights, chosen by the county, "to consider what aid they would give the King in his great necessity"; eleven years later the Parliament summoned by Simon de Montfort contained not only two knights from each county, but also two citizens from each city and two burgesses from each borough. The Parliaments of the thirteenth century were very different from those of today and, no doubt, there were even greater differences in the manner of their election. Nevertheless, a statute approved by the Parliament of Edward I, in 1275, stipulating that the elections should be "free" is still in force today, and the gradual evolution of the present system can be traced back through hundreds of Acts of Parliament spanning the centuries in between.

This evolution is a continuing process—in 1963 alone, for instance, two important changes were made—peers were permitted to vote and to stand for election if they disclaimed their titles, and the rights of servicemen to obtain a discharge to become Parliamentary candidates were restricted.[1] In fact, the two most distinctive features of the British electoral system are its antiquity and its capacity to absorb changes. While some parts of the electoral law remain intact for centuries, others are liable to be amended at virtually any time. The great majority of amendments are of a minor character.

The period of most significant change was, of course, the hundred or so years following the passage of the Great Reform Bill of 1832 when, as described briefly in Chapter 3 above, the struggle for universal suffrage was fought and won. Almost as important as the extension of the franchise, was such legislation as the Ballot Act of 1872, which secured the secrecy of the ballot, and the Corrupt Practices Act of 1883, which effectively eliminated bribery from British elections.

The advances won in the nineteenth and early twentieth centuries were consolidated in the Representation of the People Acts of 1948

[1] See pp. 64–65, above.

and 1949, which form the basis of the present system.[2] Changes in the law since 1949 have all been in a minor key, seeking to improve the detailed working of an established system rather than to effect any radical alteration. A typical example was the Elections (Welsh Forms) Act of 1964, which provided that Welsh translations of election forms could be used in Wales and Monmouthshire. Less typical, because its motivation was partisan advantage, was the Representation of the People (Amendment) Act of 1958 which, as described in Chapter 8 above, removed the restriction on the use of motor-cars prescribed by the 1948 Act.

Fairly frequent attempts are made by MPs to introduce changes through Private Members' Bills. The great majority of these attempts are unsuccessful. Examples are the repeated efforts of Conservative MPs to extend the provisions for postal voting with the obvious, if undeclared, aim of improving their own party's electoral prospects,[3] and the attempt of a Labour Member, Denis Coe, to enable party labels to be included on the ballot paper.[4]

The 1948 and 1949 Acts, although they introduced a number of important innovations, are basically nineteenth century in form, and the legal provisions relating to elections are in many respects similar to those in force one hundred years ago. What has transformed election campaigns out of all recognition in the past century has primarily been not the change in the law but the technological and sociological developments which have taken place. It would be pointless to elaborate on them in a work of this kind, but it may be useful just to list the four changes which appear to have had the greatest effect upon British elections.

First, there has been the revolution in transportation, which has enabled politicians to travel rapidly round the country—the growth of railways in the mid-nineteenth century and, even more important, the spread of the motor-car, which has also greatly affected local campaigning. In a densely populated but geographically small country, however, the aeroplane and the helicopter have, so far, made little impact upon electioneering.

[2] Though the official *Index to the Statutes in Force* (London, HMSO, 1966) lists a total of 27 statutes under "Representation of the People" which are still applicable. They extend from 1829 c.7 (Roman Catholic Relief) to 1964 c.48 (Police). Additional statutes are listed under "House of Commons: elections," beginning with 1275 c.5 (Free Elections).

[3] See, for example, the Postal and Proxy Voting Bill (introduced by Sir Ronald Russell), Second Reading Debate, House of Commons Hansard, 24 June, 1966.

[4] See House of Commons Hansard, 12 June, 1967.

Second, has been the development of mass media of communication—newspapers with national circulations, telegraphs, radio and, later, television. More humbly, the telephone has also made an incalculable contribution, though, because of the relatively small proportion of households with telephones, rather less than in certain other countries.[5] Third has been the spread of education, which again has tended to lag behind some other developed countries, especially in so far as higher education is concerned, and, finally, the development of highly centralized party machines.

In a number of respects electoral law has failed to take account of these developments. It is especially deficient, as we have seen, in its failure to mention television, to provide any control over expenditure other than in support of individual candidatures during the final campaign period, or to permit the use of party labels on ballot papers. Governments have been inhibited from legislating on these matters through fear of being accused of acting partially, but pressure, not least from the broadcasting authorities who are intensely unhappy about the legally ambiguous status of their election broadcasts, has gradually convinced the politicians that something should be done.

Fortunately, a fairly recent tradition has been established that an attempt at all-party agreement should precede any important changes in electoral law, and inter-party conferences under the chairmanship of the Speaker of the House of Commons had preceded the Representation of the People Acts of 1918 and 1948 (though in each case the Act did not exactly follow the recommendations of the Speaker's Conference.[6])

Following this precedent, shortly after the 1964 general election the new Prime Minister, Harold Wilson, invited the Speaker to preside over a conference on electoral law, and on 12 May 1965 the Speaker informed the House of Commons that he had agreed to do so. Apart from the Speaker, twenty-nine Members of Parliament, whose names were suggested by the party whips, made up the conference. The MPs were appointed in approximate proportion to party membership of the House of Commons; fifteen were Labour, thirteen Conservative and one Liberal.

[5] The number of telephones per 100 population in the UK in 1962 was 16.25. This was well behind the United States, 41.8, Sweden, 38.5, Canada, 33.2, New Zealand, 32.37 and Switzerland, 31.9. At that time, however, Britain led most of her West European neighbours—Netherlands, 14.8, West Germany 11.5, France 10.07, Italy, 8.53, Spain, 6.3. *The World's Telephones* (New York, American Telephone and Telegraph Co., 1964).

[6] See J. F. S. Ross, *Elections and Electors, op. cit.*, pp. 295–373. Another Speaker's Conference, in 1929–30, proved abortive.

The terms of reference of the Conference were as follows:

To examine and, if possible, to submit agreed resolutions on the following matters relating to Parliamentary elections:

(a) Reform of the franchise, with particular reference to the minimum age for voting and registration procedure generally;
(b) Methods of election, with particular reference to preferential voting;
(c) Conduct of elections, with particular reference to:
    (i) the problem of absent voting generally;
    (ii) use of the official mark on ballot papers and of electoral numbers on counterfoils;
    (iii) polling hours;
    (iv) appointment of polling day as a public holiday;
    (v) provisions relating to undue influence; and
    (vi) returning officers for county constituencies;
(d) Election expenses generally;
(e) Use of broadcasting; and
(f) Cost of election petitions and applications for relief.

The Conference allowed a period of time for interested organizations or individuals to submit representations, and in November 1965 began its considerations. In view of the narrow Parliamentary majority an early general election was anticipated and the Conference agreed to submit interim reports on a number of urgent matters on which early legislation might be practicable.

Three such reports were produced between 28 December 1965 and 7 March 1966,[7] but the dissolution of Parliament on 10 March prevented any action before the 1966 general election. The interim reports contained two important recommendations. By sixteen votes to eight it was agreed that the limit on election expenses should be raised by £300 per constituency and, on the Speaker's casting vote, it was recommended that there should not be a change to two election registers annually. The Conference asked the government to make a feasibility study on the use of computer techniques in compiling and keeping up to date the electoral register. It also recommended that "Y" voters (see p. 12 above) should have the date of their twenty-first birthday shown on the register and that they should be qualified to vote in any election held on or after that date. There were also a number of minor modifications recommended in the law on absent voting and on the registration of merchant seamen.

After the general election of 1966 the membership of the Con-

[7] *Conference on Electoral Law*, Cmnd. 2880, 2917, 2932 (1966), (London, HMSO, 1966).

ference was reconstituted to take account of the changes in party strengths and the defeat or retirement of some of its members. The revised Conference consisted of sixteen Labour Members, twelve Conservatives and one Liberal.

The next report from the Conference, which appeared in February 1967,[8] was almost entirely negative in its recommendations. It was not surprising that, having devoted four meetings to discussing proportional representation and the alternative vote, it decided to recommend no change: a proposal by the sole Liberal Member to introduce the single transferable vote system was defeated by 19 votes to one. Less predictable was the decision not to recommend the extension of absent voting facilities to electors on holiday. As this had previously been put forward on several occasions in Private Member's Bills sponsored by Conservative MPs, it was surprising that none of the Tories in the Conference pressed the question to a division.

Other proposals which the Conference rejected without any recorded disagreement were compulsory voting, the right to object to names included in the absent voters list, postal votes for the over-70s and special arrangements for persons admitted to hospital after the last day for claiming absent voting facilities.

The most controversial recommendations of the Conference were those contained in its fifth report, issued in May 1967.[9] By nine votes to five, it agreed that "There should be no broadcast, or publication in a newspaper or other periodical, of the result of a public opinion poll or of betting odds on the likely result of a parliamentary election during the period of seventy-two hours before the close of the poll." This proposal, which was greeted with incredulity by the pollsters themselves and by most political commentators, presumably reflected belief by MPs in the bandwagon theory, discussed on page 137 above.

Other recommendations of the Conference which were sharply criticized were that party labels should continue to be omitted from ballot papers, and that there should be no restriction on political expenditure outside the actual campaign period. That this is a field bristling with difficulties cannot be denied, but other democratic countries, including West Germany, have not been deterred from seeking a solution. As most people would agree that this expenditure is now much more important than that spent in the final weeks of the campaign, it seems pointless to continue to restrict the latter without even considering any control over the former.[10]

[8] *Conference on Electoral Law*, Cmnd. 3202 (London, HMSO, 1967).

[9] *Conference on Electoral Law*, Cmnd. 3275 (London, HMSO, 1967).

[10] See article by the present author in *Socialist Commentary*, July 1967, for a detailed critique of the recommendations of the Conference.

One field, however, in which the Conference's recommendations were generally welcomed was broadcasting. Here its proposals would have the effect of regularizing the existing position, and would go far towards removing the ambiguity which has hitherto affected political broadcasting.[11] The recommendations of the Conference are:

Broadcasting should be exempted from the provisions relating to election expenses in section 63 of the Representation of the People Act 1949; but a programme covering an election in a particular constituency and including candidates in that constituency should not be broadcast unless all the candidates have agreed to take part personally and are given an equal opportunity to state their views.

While the existing arrangements governing the allocation of time for political broadcasting at general elections are broadly satisfactory, the broadcasting authorities should review the arrangements made for broadcasts at election times by minor parties.

Section 80(1) of the Act of 1949 should be extended so as to prevent television stations outside the United Kingdom from transmitting any matter with intent to influence voters at an election; and the exception in respect of arrangements made with the British broadcasting Corporation should also apply to the Independent Television Authority and all their programme contractors.

The fifth report also contained a long list of proposals which the Conference had declined to recommend. These included the designation of polling day as a public holiday, a requirement that employees should be given time off work in order to vote, that by-elections should be held within a certain time of a vacancy occurring, that candidates' expenses should be met out of public funds and that the amount of the candidate's deposit or the proportion of votes required to save it should be amended. In a letter to the Prime Minister accompanying this report, the Speaker indicated that the only item still to be considered was the minimum age of voting. The final report, which is expected to advise a reduction from 21 to 18, will probably appear early in 1968.

When the Conference has completed its work it will be the government's responsibility to introduce a Bill, taking account of its recommendations though not necessarily following them in every detail. After this Bill has been considered by Parliament it is unlikely that there will be any further general review of electoral law for many years to come.

[11] See pp. 102–4, above.

APPENDIX I

General Election Results, 1945–1966

Table 30

Year	Parties	Candidates	MPs elected	Unopposed returns	Lost deposits	Total vote	Percentage vote
1945	Conservative	624	213	2	6	9,988,306	39·8
	Labour	604	393	1	2	11,995,152	47·8
	Liberal	306	12	—	64	2,248,226	9·0
	Others	148	22	—	91	854,294	2·8
Turn-out: 72·7% Swing (to Lab.)* 11·3%		1,682	640	3	163	25,085,978	100·0
1950	Conservative	620	298	2	5	12,502,567	43·5
	Labour	617	315	—	—	13,266,592	46·1
	Liberal	475	9	—	319	2,621,548	9·1
	Others	156	3	—	137	381,964	1·3
Turn-out: 84·0% Swing (to Con.)* 2·8%		1,868	625	2	461	28,772,671	100·0
1951	**Conservative**	617	321	4	3	13,717,538	48·0
	Labour	617	295	—	1	13,948,605	48·8
	Liberal	109	6	—	66	730,556	2·5
	Others	23	3	—	26	198,969	0·7
Turn-out: 82·5% Swing (to Con.)* 0·9%		1,376	625	4	96	28,595,668	100·0

1955	**Conservative**	623	344	—	3	13,286,569	49·7
	Labour	620	277	—	1	12,404,970	46·4
	Liberal	110	6	—	60	722,405	2·7
	Others	56	3	—	36	346,554	1·2
Turn-out	76·7%	1,409	630	—	100	26,760,493	100·0
Swing (to Con.)*	2·1%						
1959	**Conservative**	625	365	—	2	13,749,830	49·4
	Labour	621	258	—	1	12,215,538	43·8
	Liberal	216	6	—	55	1,638,571	5·9
	Others	74	1	—	58	255,302	0·9
Turn-out:	78·8%	1,536	630	—	116	27,859,241	100·0
Swing (to Con.)*	1·1%						
1964	Conservative	629	303	—	5	12,001,396	43·4
	Labour	628	317	—	8	12,205,814	44·1
	Liberal	365	9	—	53	3,092,878	11·2
	Others	135	1	—	121	348,914	1·3
Turn-out:	77·0%	1,757	630	—	187	27,649,002	100·0
Swing (to Lab.)*	3·1%						
1966	Conservative	629	253	—	9	11,418,413	41·9
	Labour	621	363	—	3	13,056,659	47·9
	Liberal	311	12	—	104	2,327,470	8·5
	Others	146	2	—	121	456,909	1·7
Turn-out:	75·8%	1,707	630	—	237	27,259,743	100·0
Swing (to Lab.)*	2·6%						

*The swing shown here is calculated on the total national vote, *not* on the average of the swings in all constituencies contested.

APPENDIX 2

Election Statistics, 1966

Electors	35,957,245
Postal voters	617,483
Polling districts	30,470
Polling stations	49,565
Members	630
Candidates	1,707
Candidates' expenses	£
Personal expenses	66,136
Agents	82,856
Clerks	46,449
Printing	762,706
Public meetings	33,046
Committee rooms	49,461
Miscellaneous matters	96,228
Total (excluding personal exps.)	1,070,746
Votes polled	27,264,747

Source: *Return of the Expenses of each Candidate at the General Election of March 1966*, House of Commons Paper 162, August 1966.

APPENDIX 3

Proxy and Postal Voters

The following categories of registered voters may claim the right to appoint *proxies* to vote on their behalf:

An elector who is likely to be at sea, or abroad, on account of his employment or on account of his service in the auxiliary or reserve forces at the time. (**RPF 10A**)

All service voters. (**F/VOTE/33**)

Wives of servicemen abroad. (**F/VOTE/34**)

Voters employed in the service of the Crown in a post outside the United Kingdom. (**ESTAVOTE**)

Wives of Crown servants residing outside the United Kingdom with their husbands. (**ESTASUFFRAGE**)

Applications to appoint a proxy must be made, on an appropriate form, at least twelve days before polling day (excluding Sundays and public holidays). The names of the forms required are given in brackets after each category. RPF forms are obtainable from the constituency returning officer (*i.e.*, at the local town hall); service forms from commanding officers, and forms for Crown servants and their wives from their own government departments. Would-be voters by proxy about to go abroad are advised to apply to appoint their proxy within six weeks before their departure. Two proxies are named on the form, the second of whom would be entitled to vote on behalf of the elector only if the first proxy indicates within five days of being approached by the returning officer that he is unable to act on behalf of the absent voter. A proxy records the vote at the same polling station at which the absent voter would otherwise be entitled to vote.

Postal votes may be claimed for an *indefinite* period by those unable, or unlikely to be able, to go to vote in person, because of:

(1) The general nature of their employment, service or occupation (for example, long-distance lorry drivers and merchant seamen). (**RPF 7**)

(2) Blindness or other physical incapacity (a doctor's signature is needed on the application form). (**RPF 7**)

(3) No longer residing at the qualifying address (unless they still reside in the same borough, urban district or rural parish). (**RPF** 8)
(4) Having to make a journey by sea or air in order to be able to vote in person. (This applies mostly to Scottish electors who live on islands away from a polling station.) (**RPF** 7A)

In addition, a postal vote may be claimed for a *particular election only*, by reason of:

(1) Service as a member of the reserve or auxiliary forces. (**RPF** 9)
(2) Employment on date of poll as a constable, or by the returning officer. (**RPF** 9)
(3) At a general election being a candidate or a candidate's spouse in some other constituency. (**RPF** 9)
(4) At a general election being a returning officer, deputy returning officer or acting returning officer, or being employed by a returning officer, in some other constituency. (**RPF** 9)

A service voter serving in the U.K., even though he has appointed a proxy, may apply to vote by post (F/VOTE/35), or may vote at his polling station personally if a ballot paper has not already been issued to his proxy.

Any proxy voter who himself falls into one of the above categories may apply to vote by post.

APPENDIX 4

Postal Votes in 1966 General Election

In the 1966 general election the postal vote exceeded the majority in twenty-four seats, won by the Conservatives. It seems probable that in about half of these constituencies this factor alone accounted for the Conservative victory.

Table 31

	Constituency	*Conservative majority*	*Number of postal votes*
1.	Peterborough	3	1,358
2.	Edinburgh, Pentlands	44	793
3.	Norfolk South	119	1,692
4.	Burton	277	1,139
5.	Holland with Boston	316	712
6.	Lowestoft	358	1,569
7.	Plymouth, Devonport	319	1,196
8.	Maldon	506	1,951
9.	Mitcham	528	717
10.	Merton and Morden	420	670
11.	Wallasey	589	1,036
12.	Ayr	484	880
13.	Hertford	794	1,201
14.	Southend East	517	1,050
15.	Eastleigh	701	1,176
16.	Hornsey	615	1,263
17.	Croydon North East	588	658
18.	Chippenham	694	1,299
19.	Hendon North	600	1,045
20.	Bath	800	1,557
21.	Colchester	1,015	1,740
22.	Norfolk South West	775	1,921
23.	Stroud	1,545	1,613
24.	Ulster, Mid	2,560	5,000

At Chippenham the candidate in second place was a Liberal, and at Mid Ulster, a Republican. In the remaining twenty-two seats the second place was secured by the Labour candidate.

APPENDIX 5

Election Timetable

The following chart lists the important days to remember during a general election campaign. It is important to remember to exclude Sundays and bank holidays in the count of seventeen days between the Proclamation and polling day.

Table 32

General election	
Day	
0.	Proclamation
1.	Receipt of writ
2.	
3.	Notice of election
4.	First day for Nomination
5.	Last day to claim proxy or postal votes
6.	
7.	
8.	Last day for Nomination
9.	
10.	
11.	
12.	
13.	
14.	
15.	
16.	
17.	Polling day

			Example
Chart days	*Calendar dates*		
0	F	5	Proclamation
1	S	6	Receipt of Writ
—	Su	7	
2	M	8	
3	T	9	Notice of Election
4	W	10	First day for Nomination
5	T	11	Last day to claim proxy or postal votes
6	F	12	
7	S	13	
—	Su	14	
8	M	15	Last day for Nomination
9	T	16	
10	W	17	
11	T	18	
12	F	19	
13	S	20	
—	Su	21	
14	M	22	
15	T	23	
16	W	24	
17	T	25	Polling day

In a by-election, the returning officer is allowed some discretion in his choice of polling day, as the following table shows.

Table 33

By-election

County	*Day*	*Borough*	*Day*
Receipt of Writ	1	Receipt of Writ	1
	2		2
Notice of Election	3	Notice of Election	3
	4		4
	5		5
	6	Earliest final Nom.	6
Earliest final Nom.	7		7
	8	Latest final Nom.	8
	9		9
Latest final Nom.	10		10
	11		11
	12		12
	13	Earliest Poll	13
Earliest Poll	14		14
	15		15
	16		16
	17	Latest Poll	17
	18		
Latest Poll	19		

APPENDIX 6

Corrupt and Illegal Practices

Table 34

SUMMARY OF

CORRUPT

Offences

BRIBERY.—No gift, loan, or promise of money or money's worth must be made to a voter to induce him either to vote or abstain from voting.

The offer or promise of a situation or employment to a voter or anyone connected with him, if made with the same object, is also bribery.

The consequences are the same whether bribery is committed before, during, or after an election.

Giving or paying money for the purpose of bribery is equivalent to the offence itself.

A gift or promise to a third person to procure a vote is bribery. Payment for loss of time, wages, or travelling expenses is equal to bribery.

Any person who receives a bribe, or bargains for employment or reward in consideration of his vote, is guilty of bribery.

TREATING.—No meat, drinks, entertainment or provisions can be paid for or provided for any person at any time, in order to induce him, or any other person, to vote or abstain from voting. The gift of tickets to be exchanged for refreshment is regarded as treating.

Treating the wives or relatives of voters is also forbidden.

The receiver of any meat, drink, etc., is equally guilty, and liable to the same consequences.*

UNDUE INFLUENCE.—No force, threat, restraint, or fraud may be used to compel an elector to vote or abstain.

Using or threatening any spiritual or temporal injury is indue influence.

The withdrawal of custom, or a threat to do so, comes under this prohibition. A threat to evict a tenant will also be undue influence.

UNAUTHORIZED EXPENDITURE.—Incurring expenditure on account of holding public meetings or issuing advertisements, circulars or publications, by any person, other than the election agent, for the purpose of promoting or procuring the election of any candidate at a Parliamentary election, unless authorized in writing by such election agent and returned as an expense by the person incurring it.

PERSONATION.—Applying for a ballot paper in the name of another person, whether alive or dead.

Voting twice in the same constituency at the same election.

Aiding or abetting the commission of the offence of personation.

Forging or counterfeiting a ballot paper.

ELECTION OFFENCES

PRACTICES

Penalties

Twelve months' imprisonment, or a fine of £200.

Deprivation of the right of voting for five years.

Removal from, and disqualification for, any public office.

Payment of costs of an election inquiry in certain cases.

If committed by the candidate he also loses his seat, if elected, and is disqualified for ten years from representing the constituency and is disqualified for five years from sitting for any other constituency.

If committed by any agent the election is void, and the candidate is disqualified for five years.

NOTE.—Any recognized active worker may be held to be "an agent."

Two years' imprisonment.

Five years' incapacity to vote, or hold any public office.

If committed by any agent, the candidate loses his seat.

Table 34—continued

ILLEGAL

Offences

CONVEYANCE.—Paying or receiving money for conveyance of votes to or from the poll.

(Private conveyances lent gratuitously can alone be employed; hackney carriages are prohibited except when hired by voters for their own exclusive use.)

ADVERTISING.—Paying money to an elector for exhibiting bills, etc. The receiver is also guilty.

VOTING when prohibited, or inducing a prohibited elector to vote.

FALSE STATEMENT.—Publishing a false statement of the withdrawal of any candidate or as to his character.

ILLEGAL PROXY VOTING.—Voting or attempting to vote in person after having appointed a proxy, and while such appointment is uncancelled.

Voting or attempting to vote as proxy on behalf of more than two absent voters at an election in any constituency, unless voting as the husband or wife, or the parent, brother or sister of the absent voter.

Voting or attempting to vote at any election under the authority of a proxy paper when the person knows or has reasonable grounds for supposing that the proxy paper has been cancelled, or that the elector on whose behalf it has been issued is dead or not entitled to vote at that election.

POLL CARDS.—Issuing at a Parliamentary election any poll card or document resembling an official poll card.

PUBLISHING BILLS, placards or posters, without the printer's name and address. (The election agent alone, or sub-agents in counties, may issue any printed matter at the election.) Any process for multiplying copies of a document other than by copying it by hand is deemed to be printing.

ILLEGAL PAYMENT, EMPLOY-

PAYMENT FOR BANDS OF MUSIC, torches, flags, banners.

LENDING OR USING, for the conveyance of voters, **horses or vehicles usually kept for hire.**

EMPLOYMENT of any person as a canvasser.

USING A COMMITTEE ROOM in any licensed house, refreshment house, or public elementary school.

***NOTE**

REFRESHMENT FOR WORKERS.—Whilst it is much better, and more prudent, to leave all workers, whether paid or unpaid, to find their own refreshments, the view has been expressed by some judges that "the giving

PRACTICES

Penalties

A fine of £100.
Incapacity to vote for five years.
If committed by a candidate or an agent, the election may be rendered void.

If the offender be the candidate or his agent, the full penalty attaching to an illegal practice as above.
If any other person, a fine not exceeding £100.

MENT, AND HIRING

A fine of £100.

---

of refreshments to persons employed at the election, if *bona fide* and honestly done, **is not treating,** even though the workers be voters, if care be taken to confine it to persons actually engaged on the election."

APPENDIX 7

Occupations of Candidates and MPs, 1966

Table 35

Occupation	Conservative Elected	Conservative Defeated	Labour Elected	Labour Defeated	Liberal Elected	Liberal Defeated
Professions						
Barrister	55	46	36	9	3	20
Solicitor	15	37	18	13	—	23
Doctor, Dentist	2	6	9	2	1	6
Architect/Surveyor	2	6	1	5	—	8
Civil Engineer	1	6	3	5	—	3
Chartered Secretary/Accountant	6	25	5	2	1	11
Civil Servant, Local Govt.	13	17	9	13	—	10
Armed Services	19	16	3	—	—	7
Teaching						
University	1	5	24	9	—	10
Adult	—	2	15	27	—	10
School	3	14	33	45	1	36
Total	117	180	156	130	6	144
Business						
Small Business	2	12	2	2	—	9
Company Director	40	44	3	3	1	28
Company Executive	12	56	11	23	2	27
Commerce, Insurance	16	25	13	4	—	21
Management, Clerical	5	7	3	11	—	6
Total	75	44	32	43	3	91
Miscellaneous						
Miscellaneous "white collar"	7	7	22	34	—	17
Private means	5	—	—	—	—	—
Politician	2	4	9	7	1	2
Publicists, Journalists	17	19	29	14	—	22
Farmer	27	15	2	3	2	13
Housewife	1	1	4	2	—	3
Student	—	—	—	2	—	2
Total	59	46	66	62	3	59
Workers						
Railway clerks	—	1	9	—	—	—
Miners	—	—	32	3	—	—
Skilled	2	5	47	19	—	5
Semi- and unskilled	—	—	21	1	—	—
Total	2	6	109	23	—	5
Grand total	253	376	363	258	12	299

(Reprinted from *The British General Election of 1966*, *op. cit.*, pp. 208–9.)

APPENDIX 8

Opinion Poll Constituency Surveys, 1966

In the 1966 general election opinion poll surveys were undertaken in fifty-five constituencies. The margin of error for each survey is shown below (figures taken from *The Sunday Times*, 3 April 1966).

IN DETAIL: ERRORS IN CONSTITUENCY POLLS

Error in predicting gap between the two leading parties

GALLUP	
Birmingham Evening Mail	
Smethwick	2·2
Yardley	0·1
Perry Barr	0·5
Cambridge Evening News	
Cambridge	2·9
Sunday Telegraph	
Bexley	9·8
MARPLAN (random samples)	
Sunday Times	
Bexley	0·8
Kemptown	2·9
Oxford	4·5
York	3·1
Monmouth	0·3
Preston South	0·6
MARPLAN (quota sample)	
Sunday Times	
Falmouth	7·5
WESTMINSTER PRESS	
Kemptown	0·0
Devizes	17·8
Cleveland	7·2
Chippenham	9·7
Bishop Auckland	5·2
York	11·2
Tynemouth	5·4
Keighley	1·2
BIRMINGHAM PLANET	
Perry Barr	4·8
S.E. LONDON MERCURY	
Lewisham North	10·2
Lewisham West	11·0
Woolwich West	5·6
A. J. ALLEN ASSOCIATES (random samples)	
Economist	
Keighley	9·8
Tavistock	4·4
West Bromwich	4·5
Hitchin	16·8
Guardian	
York	2·0
Bolton East	0·9
Yardley	2·1
Norwood	8·7
Yarmouth	10·2
Watford	8·8
Pollock	4·1
Eastleigh	4·7
A. J. ALLEN ASSOCIATES (multiple regression)	
Birmingham Post	
Smethwick	9·3
Perry Barr	5·6
Rugby	0·5
Stroud	4·4
All Saints	4·2
Sparkbrook	13·4
Yardley	2·6
Coventry South	2·4
Oldbury	5·4
West Bromwich	9·8
Meriden	9·0
Perry Barr	4·8

EVENING STANDARD	
Billericay	2·4
Dulwich	5·3
Hampstead	0·7
Ealing North	1·5
Orpington	27·6

SHEFFIELD TELEGRAPH	
Sheffield Heeley	5·0
NOP (*Daily Mail*)	
Lewisham North	2·4

Average error in predictions of gap

Marplan (random samples)	2·0
NOP	2·4
Gallup	3·1
Birmingham Planet	4·8
Sheffield Telegraph	5·0
A. J. Allen Associates (multiple regression analysis)	6·1
A. J. Allen Associates (local samples)	6·4
Westminster Press	7·2
Marplan (quota sample)	7·5
Evening Standard (2·5 if Orpington excluded)	7·5
S.E. London Mercury	8·9

APPENDIX 9

Bibliography

ELECTION RESULTS. Full results of general elections, together with biographical details of Members and of defeated candidates are published shortly after each election in *The Times House of Commons*, published by *The Times* (London). The series goes back to 1929, and also appeared after the elections of January 1910, December 1910 and 1918. Full results of the 1966 election, without biographical details but with some interesting statistical analysis, are also given in *The Daily Telegraph–Gallup Analysis of the Election '66* (London, *Daily Telegraph*, 1966).

Less detailed results are given also in *Dod's Parliamentary Companion*, published annually, *Vacher's Parliamentary Guide*, quarterly and *Whitaker's Almanack*, annually.

Tabulated results for all constituencies from 1950 to 1964 inclusive are included in *British Parliamentary Election Results 1950–1964* by B. R. Mitchell and Klaus Boehm (Cambridge University Press, 1966). Summaries over a sixty-year period are included in *British Political Facts 1900–1960* by D. E. Butler and Jennie Freeman (London, Macmillan, 1963).

ACCOUNTS OF GENERAL ELECTIONS are provided by a series of books sponsored by Nuffield College, Oxford:

The British General Election of 1945 by R. B. McCallum and Alison Readman (London, Macmillan, 1947); *The British General Election of 1950* by H. G. Nicholas (London, Macmillan, 1951); *The British General Election of 1951* by D. E. Butler (London, Macmillan, 1952); *The British General Election of 1955* by D. E. Butler (London, Macmillan, 1955); *The British General Election of 1959* by D. E. Butler and Richard Rose (London, Macmillan, 1960); *The British General Election of 1964* by D. E. Butler and Anthony King (London, Macmillan, 1965); *The British General Election of 1966* by D. E. Butler and Anthony King (London, Macmillan, 1966). The 1964 campaign, and the events leading up to it, is also described in *The Making of the Prime Minister* by Anthony Howard and Richard West (London, Cape, 1965, and New York, Macmillan, 1965 (as *The Road to No. 10*)).

Campaigns in individual constituencies are described in *How People Vote* by M. Benney, A. P. Gray and R. H. Pear (London, Routledge and Kegan Paul, 1956) (Greenwich in 1950); *Straight Fight* by R. S. Milne and H. C. Mackenzie (London, Hansard Society, 1954) (Bristol, North-East in 1951); *Marginal Seat* by R. S. and H. C. Mackenzie (London, Hansard Society, 1958) (Bristol, North-East in 1955); *The General Election in Glasgow* by S. B. Chrimes (Glasgow University Press, 1950). Campaigns in a number of constituencies containing immigrant voters are described in *Colour and the British Electorate 1964*, by Nicholas Deakin (London, Pall Mall Press, 1965).

Accounts of local government election campaigns are given in *A Metropolis Votes* by L. J. Sharpe (London School of Economics, 1962) (The L.C.C. elections of 1961) and *Voting in Cities*, edited by L. J. Sharpe (London, Macmillan, 1967) (Eleven borough council elections in May 1964).

THE ELECTORAL SYSTEM. The fullest account of its recent development is *The British Electoral System since 1918* by D. E. Butler (Oxford University Press, 1963, second edition). A critical assessment is made in *Political Representation and Elections in Britain* by P. J. Pulzer (London, Allen and Unwin, 1968). An earlier study, which includes much information about alternative systems of voting, is *Elections and Electors* by J. F. S. Ross (London, Eyre and Spottiswoode, 1955). A concise discussion of the principles underlying different electoral systems is provided by *Free Elections* by W. J. M. Mackenzie (London, Allen and Unwin, 1958). Details of systems in many countries are given in *Parliaments and Electoral Systems* (London, Institute of Electoral Research, 1962) and *Voting in Democracies* by Enid Lakeman and J. D. Lambert (London, Faber, 1955).

CAMPAIGN TECHNIQUES. No general work has yet appeared. *Influencing Voters* by Richard Rose (London, Faber, 1967) analyzes the campaigns leading up to the 1964 election, and a number of campaigns are described in *Communication and Political Power* by Lord Windlesham (London, Cape, 1966). The impact of television on the 1959 general election is comprehensively examined in *Television and the Political Image* by Joseph Trenaman and Denis McQuail (London, Methuen, 1961). More recent data is discussed in *Election Television in the 1960's* by J. G. Blumler and D. McQuail (London, Faber, forthcoming).

VOTERS. The best general analyses yet to appear are *Voters, Parties, and Leaders* by J. Blondel (London, Penguin, 1963) and an essay by Mark Abrams in *Class,* edited by Richard Mabey (London, Anthony Blond, 1967). Interesting data is included in *The Middle Class Vote* by J. Bonham (London, Faber, 1954), *Angels in Marble: the working class Conservatives in England* by Robert McKenzie and Allan Silver (London, Heinemann, 1968), *The Working Class Tories* by Eric Nordlinger (London, MacGibbon and Kee, 1967) and *The English Voter* by A. J. Allen (London, English Universities Press, 1964). The first large-scale study likely to appear is *The British Voter* by D. E. Butler and Donald Stokes (London, Macmillan, forthcoming). A comparative analysis of voting behaviour in Britain, the United States, Australia and Canada is made in *Party and Society* by Robert R. Alford (New York, Rand McNally, 1963, and London, John Murray, 1964).

CANDIDATES. Two recent books on candidate selection, which cover the field comprehensively are *Pathways to Parliament* by Austin Ranney (Madison, University of Wisconsin Press, and London, Macmillan, 1965) and *The Selectorate* by Peter Paterson (London, MacGibbon and Kee, 1967). On Members of Parliament see *Honourable Members* by Peter G. Richards (London, Faber, 1964, second edition) and *The British Political Elite* by W. L. Guttsman (London, MacGibbon and Kee, 1963).

POLITICAL PARTIES. The standard work is *British Political Parties* by R. T. McKenzie (London, Heinemann, 1963, second edition). A more historical account is *The Growth of the British Party System* (two volumes) by Ivor Bulmer-Thomas (London, John Baker, 1966). On the Labour Party see *The Left* by Gerald Kaufman (London, Anthony Blond, 1967); on the Liberals, *The Liberal Party: A Study of Retrenchment and Revival* by Jorgen Scott Rasmussen (Phoenix, University of Arizona Press, 1964, and London, Constable, 1965) and *The Liberal Dilemma* by Alan Watkins (London, MacGibbon and Kee, 1966); on the Communists, *The British Communist Party* by Henry Pelling (London, Black, 1958); on minor parties, *The British Political Fringe* by George Thayer (London, Anthony Blond, 1965). The best sources of information about local political organization are *Constituency Politics: A Study of Newcastle-under-Lyme* by Frank Bealey, J. Blondel and W. P. McCann (London, Faber, 1965) and *Small Town Politics* (a study of Glossop, Derbyshire) by A. H. Birch (Oxford University Press, 1959). Details of the organization of the three main parties are given in *The Party Organization*

(Conservative Party, 1961) *Party Organization* (Labour Party, 1957) and *Effective Organizing* (Liberal Party, 1963).

POLITICAL CULTURE. The best recent descriptions are contained in *Politics in England* by Richard Rose (Boston, Little Brown and Co., 1964, and London, Faber, 1965) and *Modern British Politics* by Samuel H. Beer (London, Faber, 1965, and New York, Alfred A. Knopf, 1965 (as *British Politics in the Collectivist Age*)). Two excellent compendia of recent writings on British politics are *British Politics: People, Parties and Parliament* by Anthony King (Boston, D. C. Heath, 1966) and *Studies in British Politics* by Richard Rose (London, Macmillan, 1966).

ELECTION LAW. The standard reference books are *Parliamentary Elections* by A. Norman Schofield (London, Shaw and Sons, 1959, third edition, and Supplement, 1964); *Local Elections* by A. Norman Schofield (London, Shaw and Sons, 1962, fourth edition); *Parker's Election Agent and Returning Officer* (London, Charles Knight and Co., 1959, sixth edition) and *Sir T. Erskine May's Parliamentary Practice* (London, Butterworth, 1964, seventeenth edition).

APPENDIX 10

Glossary[1]

A list of terms, and of personalities, mentioned in the text, which may be unfamiliar to non-British readers.

Agent. Each candidate for public office must appoint an election agent who is legally responsible for the conduct of his campaign. Many constituency parties employ full-time professional agents who are responsible for party organization between election campaigns.

Alderman. Member of local government authority, chosen not by popular election but by co-option by elected councillors.

Asquith, Herbert Henry (1852–1928). Prime Minister and leader of Liberal Party, 1908–15. Premier in coalition government, 1915–16. Created Earl of Oxford and Asquith, 1925.

Attlee, Clement (1883–1967). Leader of the Labour Party, 1935–45. Prime Minister 1945–51. Created Earl Attlee, 1955.

Backbencher. Member of Parliament *not* in the government nor an official spokesman of the Opposition.

Barrister. Lawyer who argues cases in court.

BBC. British Broadcasting Corporation. State-owned corporation with a monopoly of sound radio broadcasting and control of two of the three television channels.

Bevan, Aneurin (1897–1960). Deputy leader of Labour Party, 1959–60. Minister in Attlee government who resigned in 1951 over the government's budgetary policy and subsequently led left-wing faction of Labour Party.

Bevin, Ernest (1881–1951). Secretary of State for Foreign Affairs, 1945–51. Minister of Labour, 1940–45 in wartime coalition government. Formerly general secretary of Transport and General Workers Union.

Block vote. Vote cast at Labour Party annual conference by trade unions; each union's entire delegation voting as a bloc.

Borough council. Local government body in a large or medium sized town.

Brown, George (1914–). Foreign Secretary since 1966. Deputy leader of Labour Party since November 1960. Defeated by Harold Wilson for the leadership of Labour Party in January 1963.

[1] Compiled by Norma Percy.

Butler, Richard Austin (1902–). Senior Conservative Cabinet Minister in Churchill, Eden, Macmillan and Douglas-Home governments. Unsuccessful candidate for leader of party in 1957 and 1963. Created Lord Butler, 1965.

By-election. Election held in an individual constituency to fill a Parliamentary vacancy between general elections. Also an election to fill a casual vacancy on a local government body.

Callaghan, James (1912–). Chancellor of the Exchequer since 1964. Defeated by Harold Wilson for leadership of Labour Party in January 1963.

Campbell-Bannerman, Sir Henry (1836–1908). Leader of the Liberal Party in the House of Commons, 1899–1908. Prime Minister 1905–8.

Canvass. Door-to-door inquiry carried out by party activists to provide a reliable record of the electorate's voting intentions.

Central Office. National headquarters of the Conservative Party. Generally used as a shorthand for the party's national organization.

Constituency. Electoral district returning one Member of Parliament. (Equivalent to a Congressional District.)

Count, the. Enumeration of ballots after the polls close.

Counting agent. Supporter of a candidate deputed to watch the election officials count the votes. Also known as scrutineer.

County Council. Elected local government body for county areas.

Daily Express—also **Sunday Express.** Popular newspaper with large circulation and Conservative sympathies.

Daily Mirror. Popular tabloid newspaper. Generally pro-Labour.

Daily Sketch. Popular tabloid newspaper. Pro-Conservative.

Daily Telegraph—also **Sunday Telegraph.** Quality newspaper with Conservative sympathies.

Disraeli, Benjamin, Lord Beaconsfield (1804–81). Conservative Prime Minister, 1868 and 1874–80. Also novelist and Conservative political theorist.

Dissolution. Termination of a Parliament by the Monarch on the advice of the Prime Minister, prior to a general election.

Douglas-Home, Sir Alec (1903–). Earl of Home, 1951–63. Foreign Secretary, 1960–63. Renounced his peerage to succeed Harold Macmillan as Prime Minister and leader of Conservative Party. Prime Minister, 1963–64. Resigned as Conservative leader, July 1965.

Election address. Leaflet produced by each candidate containing biographical information and points from the party platform. Sent to each voter during the campaign.

Election writ. Legal document issued to authorize an election.

Endorsement. Candidates, although selected locally, must be approved, or endorsed, by their national party.

Freehold, leasehold. Property terms—owners of the land hold the freehold, while those who rent it for a fixed period hold the leasehold.
Gaitskell, Hugh (1906–63). Chancellor of the Exchequer, 1950–51. Leader of the Labour Party, 1955–63.
General election. Parliamentary elections, held at the discretion of the Prime Minister at less than five-yearly intervals, in which the entire House of Commons, including Ministers, stand for election.
Gordon Walker, Patrick (1907–). Labour politician. Foreign Secretary, October 1964 to January 1965, when defeated at a by-election at Leyton. Rejoined Wilson Cabinet in January 1965.
Granada. One of the independent television companies, broadcasting in the north of England.
Grimond, Jo (1913–). Leader of Liberal Party, 1956–67.
Guardian, The. Formerly the *Manchester Guardian.* Quality daily newspaper, traditionally Liberal, but in recent years increasingly pro-Labour.
Hogg, Quintin (Lord Hailsham) (1907–). Former Conservative Cabinet Minister. Renounced his peerage to contest (unsuccessfully) the party leadership in 1963.
Heath, Edward (1916–). Leader of Conservative Party since July 1965. Leading figure in governments of Macmillan and Douglas-Home.
ITA. Independent Television Authority. Body appointed by government to supervise commercial television broadcasting by the various commercial companies.
Knocking-up. Visiting the homes of supporters on election day to urge them to vote.
MacDonald, James Ramsay (1866–1937). First Labour Prime Minister, 1924. Leader of Labour Party, 1922–31. Prime Minister of minority Labour Government, 1929–31 and of National Government, 1931–35.
Macmillan, Harold (1894–). Conservative Prime Minister 1957–63; Foreign Secretary 1955; Chancellor of the Exchequer 1955–57.
Manifesto. Party platform adopted by the national leadership of the party at the beginning of a general election campaign.
Marginal seat. Constituency which is liable to change hands at a general election because it is held by a small majority.
Maudling, Reginald (1917–). Conservative Minister 1952–64. Defeated by Edward Heath for party leadership in July 1965. Deputy leader of Conservative Party since 1965.
Maxwell-Fyfe, Sir David (Lord Kilmuir) (1900–67). Prominent

minister in post-war Conservative governments. Chairman of Maxwell-Fyfe Committee which recommended important changes in the organization of the Conservative Party.

Mosley, Sir Oswald (1896–). British Fascist leader. Formerly successively a Conservative, Independent and Labour MP. Now leads party known as the Union Movement.

MP. Abbreviation for Member of Parliament, meaning a member of the House of Commons.

News Chronicle. Popular daily newspaper, with pro-Liberal sympathies, which ceased publication in 1960.

Observer, The. Quality Sunday newspaper with left of centre views.

Parish. Small local government unit in rural areas.

Phillips, Morgan (1902–63). General secretary of Labour Party, 1944–63.

Polling day. Election day.

Polling district. Sub-division of a constituency containing all electors who vote at one polling station.

Poole, Lord (1911–). Chairman, or Deputy Chairman of Conservative Party, 1955–59 and 1963–64.

Postal vote. Absentee ballot. Available to a more restricted group of voters than in the United States.

Powell, Enoch (1912–). Conservative politician on right wing of party. Minister in Macmillan's government, but refused to join that of Sir Alec Douglas-Home in 1963. Unsuccessfully contested party leadership in 1965.

Private Member's Bill. Bill sponsored by a backbench MP as opposed to the majority of legislation which is introduced by the government.

Queen's Counsel (Q.C.). A senior barrister.

Redistribution. The realignment of boundaries of electoral districts. (U.S. redistricting.)

Regional Organizer. Party official in charge of supervising elections and constituency parties in a geographical region.

Representation of the People Acts. (Reform Bills.) A series of Acts dealing with suffrage and election law.

Returning officer. Public official appointed to supervise the conduct of an election in each individual constituency.

Rosette. Ribbons in party colours worn by party activists during an election campaign. (Cf. American campaign buttons.)

Salisbury, Fifth Marquess of (1893–). Right-wing Conservative politician. Resigned from Macmillan government in 1957.

Select Committee. Committee set up by Parliament to inquire into a specific problem.

Shadow Cabinet. The collective leadership of the opposition party. Also called Opposition Front Bench Spokesmen.
Smith Square. A square in London where the three main parties' headquarters are located. Often used to refer to these headquarters collectively.
Socialist Commentary. Intellectual monthly magazine published by right-of-centre Labour activists.
Speaker, the. Presiding officer of the House of Commons. Selected by MPs, but once chosen becomes non-partisan.
Sponsored candidate. Parliamentary candidate financially supported by a trade union or other organization affiliated to the Labour Party.
Stormont. Parliament responsible for domestic affairs in Northern Ireland.
Subscription ("Subs."). Membership fee paid to belong to a political party.
Sun, The. Popular daily newspaper with Labour sympathies. Replaced the more officially Labour *Daily Herald* in 1964.
Surgery. Doctor's clinic. Used in a political context to mean the times when an MP makes himself available to his constituents to hear their personal problems.
Swing. Average of one party's gain and the other's loss. Used by political commentators to evaluate overall change in a constituency between two elections.
Thorpe, Jeremy (1929–). Leader of Liberal Party since 1967.
Times, The. Quality daily newspaper, with mildly pro-Conservative sympathies. Often mistakenly regarded in foreign countries as official voice of the British government.
Tote. Gambling scheme used by constituency parties to raise funds.
Transport and General Workers' Union (TGWU). Britain's largest trade union. Roughly equivalent to American Teamster's Union.
Transport House. National headquarters of the Labour Party. Often used as shorthand for the Labour Party national organization. Also the headquarters of the Transport and General Workers' Union.
TUC. The Trades Union Congress. Federal body to which most of the British trade unions are affiliated. Roughly equivalent to the AFL-CIO.
Ward. Local government district in a town, electing a certain number of local councillors.
Westminster. Borough of London containing Parliament, many government offices and party national headquarters. Often used as shorthand for the British political world in general.

Whip. Member of Parliament or peer charged with organizing votes of party's Parliamentary supporters. Also refers to the letter sent to MPs by their party leadership telling them how and when to vote in the following week.

Wilson, James Harold (1916–). Prime Minister since October 1964. Leader of Labour Party since February 1963. Resigned from Attlee Government with Aneurin Bevan in 1951.

Index